Route 66 Missouri

Joe Sonderman

Schiffer Publishing Ltd

4880 Lower Valley Road, Atglen, Pennsylvania 19310

Dedication

For Lorraine, Cathy, Kim, and Matt.

Acknowledgments

Special thanks to Tommy and Glenda Pike of the Route 66 Association of Missouri, Jane Lee of the Missouri Department of Transportation, and Margie Stout. Cathy Dame of the Lebanon-Laclede County Library, and Terry Primas provided valuable assistance. No book on Route 66 would be possible without the research of Skip Curtis, Jim Powell, Jim Ross, Jerry McClanahan, and Norma Baret Bolin.

Other Schiffer Books on Related Subjects:

A Journey through Northern Arizona. Victoria Clark.
ISBN: 9780764330100. $24.99

Southern California Eats. John Eng & Adriene Biondo.
ISBN: 9780764333323. $24.99

Library of Congress Control Number: 2010929861

Designed by Stephanie Daugherty
Type set in Bernhard Modern BT/News Gothic BT

ISBN: 978-0-7643-3413-9
Printed in China

Schiffer Books are available at special discounts for bulk purchases for sales promotions or premiums. Special editions, including personalized covers, corporate imprints, and excerpts can be created in large quantities for special needs. For more information contact the publisher:

Published by Schiffer Publishing Ltd.
4880 Lower Valley Road
Atglen, PA 19310
Phone: (610) 593-1777; Fax: (610) 593-2002
E-mail: Info@schifferbooks.com

For the largest selection of fine reference books on this and related subjects, please visit our web site at **www.schifferbooks.com**
We are always looking for people to write books on new and related subjects. If you have an idea for a book please contact us at the above address.

This book may be purchased from the publisher. Include $5.00 for shipping. Please try your bookstore first. You may write for a free catalog.

In Europe, Schiffer books are distributed by
Bushwood Books
6 Marksbury Ave.
Kew Gardens
Surrey TW9 4JF England
Phone: 44 (0) 20 8392 8585; Fax: 44 (0) 20 8392 9876
E-mail: info@bushwoodbooks.co.uk
Website: www.bushwoodbooks.co.uk

Contents

Introduction

Route 66 is arguably the most famous road in the world. But it was never just a road. Roads take you to a destination. Route 66 is a destination. It's for those who think that getting there is at least half the fun. You don't experience anything blasting through the landscape at 75 miles per hour in air-conditioned, cruise-controlled comfort, distracted by stereos, DVD players, and video games. The same generic chain motels and fast food restaurants are clustered at each freeway exit. If you want to savor life, it begins at the Interstate 44 off ramp.

You could make a case that the most historically significant sections of Route 66 are in Oklahoma, or the most scenic section is in Arizona. But since I'm from the "Show Me State," you would have a hard time convincing *me* that Missouri isn't the best of the eight states that can boast a stretch of Route 66. Springfield can lay claim to being the birthplace of Route 66. A Missouri attraction became the most famous of the tourist stops along the highway. A motel in St. Louis became one of the most notorious. A traveler headed west on Route 66 left the plains of Illinois behind, crossing the mightiest of America's rivers. Passing through the largest city on the route between Chicago and LA, the motorist soon found him- or herself in the rolling hills of the Ozark Plateau. West of Springfield, the land flattens out, and the traveler begins to realize he or she is headed into the great American West.

In many cases, postcards were the only way the small businesses, mom and pop motels and eateries, were ever documented. For travelers, they were the best way to send a message and show the folks back home what they were missing. They also served as a way to brag about how many miles the old family truckster had traveled that day, or lament about car troubles, the weather or a lousy tourist court. They now provide a snapshot in time. Route 66 is history you can still experience, and postcards are one way to find out what is was like to travel before we were all in such a big hurry.

History of Missouri's Route 66

Hundreds of years before computerized, climate controlled, metal cocoons roared across Missouri, the Osage Indians blazed footpaths between the Ozarks and the confluence of the Missouri and Mississippi Rivers. Cherokee Indians forced to move from the southeastern U.S. to Oklahoma made the bitter journey on the "Trail of Tears" along part of this route in the 1830s.

The first official recognition of the future Route 66 by the state came in 1835. A road was authorized "from the city of St. Louis to the City of Jefferson by the way of Manchester and Union" (later part of U.S. 66 and U.S. 50). On February 6, 1837, a state road was authorized between St. Louis and Springfield. In 1858, the federal government strung telegraph lines along the route, soon dubbed "The Telegraph Road" or "Wire Road." It was a vital military thoroughfare during the Civil War. The railroads dominated travel after the war, and Missouri's rutted and muddy roads were simply for local travel or a connection to the nearest railroad station. Road construction and maintenance were strictly local issues.

There were enough automobiles by 1903 that Missouri began charging $2 annually for a state auto license, with the money used for roads. The state appointed a State Highway Engineer in 1907 under the Board of Agriculture to help counties with roads. That position was eliminated when the State Highway Department was created in 1913. In 1917, the Hawes Law created a state road fund from registration fees and federal dollars, launching the modern era of state road building in Missouri.

Meanwhile, promoters were painting color-coded stripes on fence posts, telegraph poles or any handy surface. They gave their roads colorful names, such as the Lincoln Highway, Dixie Highway, or Old Spanish Trail. In 1917, an association mapped out the Ozark Trail from St. Louis to Romeroville, New Mexico, where it joined the National Old Trails Road to Los Angeles. Most of these promoters made money from "contributions" by merchants to have the highway routed past their doors, often taking the hapless motorist miles out of their way. By 1924, there were over 250 such trails in the U.S., promoted by at least 100 different groups, each using their own symbols and colored markings.

Near Lebanon, 1920s. ***Missouri Department of Transportation***

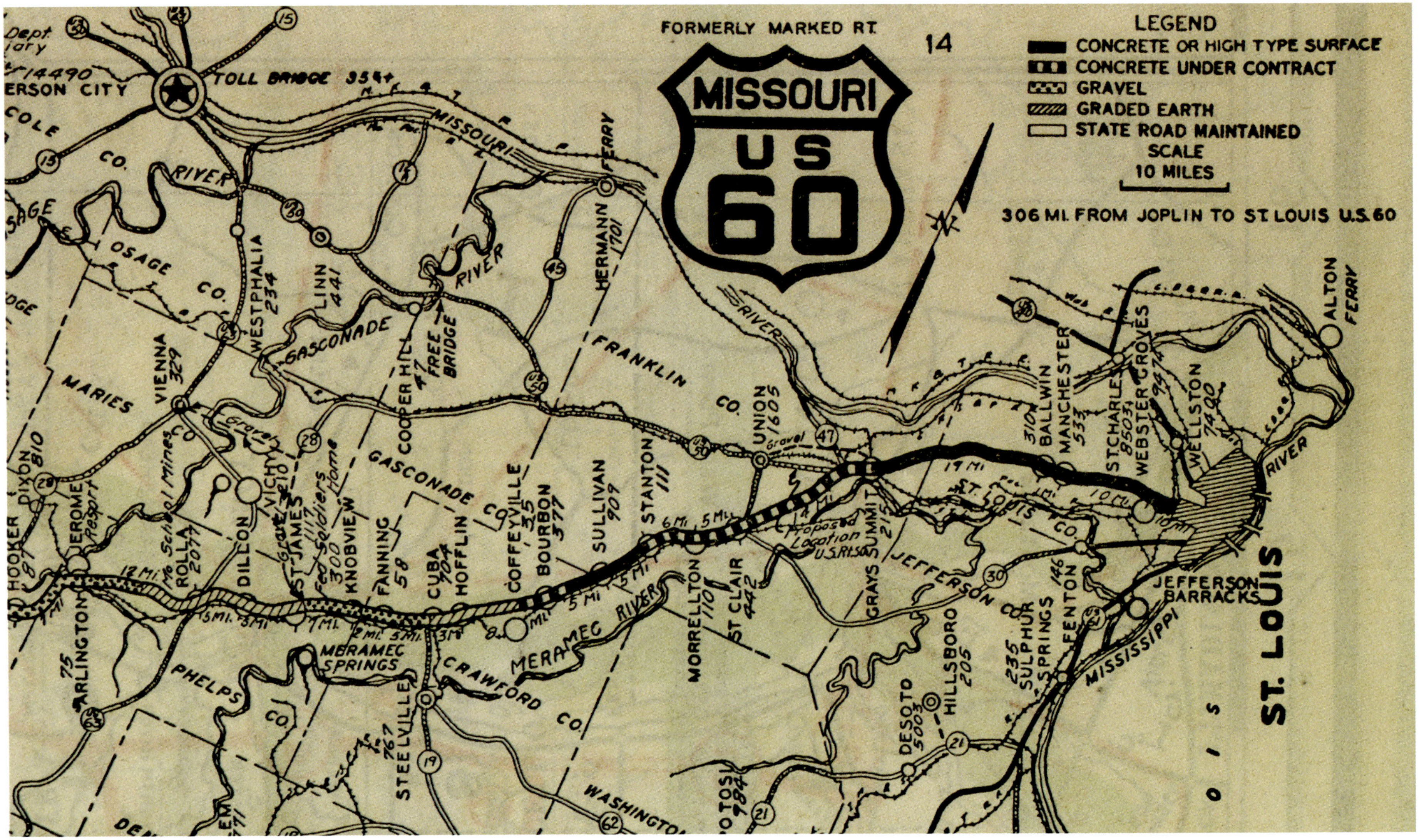

Official Missouri Highway Map. ***Author's collection*** **(1926, $25-30)**

Missouri voters took action in 1920, approving a $60 million road bond issue to "Lift Missouri Out of the Mud." The General Assembly passed the "Centennial Road Law" in 1921, designating 1,500 miles of roads connecting the principal population centers to be of a "higher type than claybound gravel." The route between St. Louis and Joplin was designated State Route 14 in September 1922.

In 1925, meeting at the Jefferson Hotel in St. Louis, The American Association of State Highway Officials approved a numbering system calling for east-west federal highways to be assigned even numbers. The north-south routes would be given odd numbers. The most important east-west routes would end in zero, and the primary north and south routes would end in one or five. The important-sounding 60 was assigned to the highway between Chicago and Los Angeles.

Maps went to press in Missouri showing Route 60 linking St. Louis and Joplin. But Kentucky Governor William J. Fields complained that no routes ending with zero passed through his state. He demanded that 60 go through Kentucky and 62 be assigned to the Chicago to Los Angeles route. That didn't set well with officials in Missouri and Oklahoma.

Cyrus Avery of Tulsa, Oklahoma, is referred to as "The Father of Route 66." He joined Missouri highway officials in putting up a fight. Finally, they noticed that the catchy sounding "66" was still unclaimed. On April 30, 1926, meeting in Springfield, they agreed to "66" for the Chicago to Los Angeles Route. The 96,000 mile Federal Highway System routes were approved on November 11, 1926.

It was good old-fashioned hype and hucksterism that set Route 66 apart right away. In 1928, C.C. "Cash and Carry" Pyle promoted a transcontinental foot race from Los Angeles to Chicago along 66, and then on to New York City! On March 4, 1928, 275 runners started in the "Bunion Derby" with the newspaper reporters in tow. Joplin leaders offered more money, so promoter C.C. Pyle went back on his agreement for the runners to stay in Carthage, opting for Joplin and Miller instead. Angry residents of Carthage pelted the lead cars with eggs. St. Louis also said "no thanks," and the caravan spent the night in East St. Louis. There were just 72 runners left when

Bunion Derby Program. ***Missouri Department of Transportation*** **(1926, $150-200)**

they crossed the Mississippi on April 27. Just 55 runners were left when a part-Cherokee Indian named Andy Payne from the Route 66 town of Foyil, Oklahoma, crossed the finish line first in the Big Apple on May 26th. Andy made the 3,400-mile run in 87 days. He won $25,000, C.C. Pyle lost a pile of money, and Route 66 reaped the publicity.

The final section of Route 66 in Missouri to be paved was near Arlington and work was completed on January 5, 1931. A few weeks later, thousands of people turned out in Rolla for a huge celebration to mark the occasion.

Businesses quickly sprang up to serve the traveler. C.H. Laessig opened the first gas station in the U.S. at 412 Theresa Street in St. Louis in 1905. In 1919, AAA opened a tourist camp in St. Louis' Forest Park. Early motorists didn't care for the finery of the big city hotels. Many derided as "tin can tourists" just camped beside the road where they pleased. It wasn't long before locals began putting up a cabin or two. Soon, there were tourist courts ranging from simple John's Modern Cabins west of Rolla to the deco splendor of the Coral Court in St. Louis.

A hit song further ingrained Route 66 into the nation's consciousness. And it was born in Missouri. Songwriter Bobby Troup was on a trip west with his wife Cynthia when she suggested he write a song about Route 40. Troup said that would be silly, since they would soon be traveling on Route 66. Just outside St. Louis, Cynthia whispered, "Get Your Kicks on Route 66." Nat King Cole recorded the song on March 16, 1946, and it just missed the top ten on the *Billboard* pop chart. Since then, it has been recorded by dozens of other artists.

The post-World War II era is considered the golden age of Route 66. Roadside hucksterism was at its height. Establishments tried hard to set themselves apart from the competition. They turned to roadside reptile ranches, basket weaving, rock curios, and even a concocted legend about Jesse James. The television series "Route 66" added to the legend.

Even as businesses along 66 reveled in the post war boom, change was already in the air. During World War Two, General Dwight David

Sheet music for *Route 66. Author's Collection* **(1946, $15-20)**

Eisenhower saw how good roads were vital for national defense. He also saw construction as a way to stimulate the economy. Congress passed his Federal Highway Aid Act in 1956. On August 2, 1956, Missouri became the first state to award a contract under the new law, for work on four-lane Route 66 in Laclede County. The nation's first actual Interstate construction took place west of the Missouri River on I-70 at St. Charles.

In 1962, as construction on the interstates continued at a breathless pace, Missouri took the lead in asking federal highway officials to designate I-66 from Chicago to Los Angeles. The request was denied and I-66 was assigned to a short stretch of highway near Washington, D.C. The towns along Route 66 between Carthage and Springfield threatened to sue to keep the U.S. 66 designation. Highway officials responded by building I-44 farther south. By 1965, those towns were completely by-passed. By 1972, Interstate 44 had replaced 66 across Missouri. Finally, in June 1974, AASHTO voted to eliminate US Route 66 from Chicago to Joplin. The Route 66 sign east of Joplin remained up until January 24, 1977, when I-55 in Illinois was brought up to Interstate standards. Joplin remained the eastern terminus on Route 66 until the entire route was decertified in 1984.

Interstate 44 replaced old 66 in Missouri, but it couldn't kill it. Drivers continued to go out of their way to connect with the people and travel through the heart of the towns instead of around them. By 1990, there was enough interest to form the Route 66 Association of Missouri, "To preserve, promote and develop old Route 66 in Missouri."

The Association led the push for a measure designating Route 66 as a historic highway through the state. Governor John Ashcroft signed the bill in July 1990. The measure cleared the way for MODOT to begin erecting signs marking the historic right of way. Today, the association and Route 66 "roadies" are dedicated to preserving the road for future generations.

Interstate 44 and U.S. 66. *Missouri Department of Transportation* **(late 1960s)**

The Icons

Of all the stops along Route 66, some stand out. These are the icons of the road, the spots known by "roadies" all around the world. They have been featured in countless books, magazine articles, movies, and T.V. shows. Missouri has more than its share of these places. Some of them exist only in our collective memories. But most are still there, waiting to be sought out by the traveler with a sense of adventure.

Ted Drewes Sr. opened his first St. Louis frozen custard stand on Natural Bridge in 1930 and a second location on South Grand in 1931. The world famous Route 66 location opened in 1941. In 1959, Ted Drewes Jr. began serving his world famous concretes, so thick they can be turned upside down.

The Chain of Rocks Bridge opened on July 20, 1929, carrying Route 66 from 1936 to 1955 and By-Pass 66 from 1955 to 1965. The Corps of Engineers demanded that the bridge face the main channel head on to prevent hindrance to navigation, making the 24 degree bend in the middle necessary for the span to come ashore on land owned by the promoters on the Missouri side. (c. 1950, $4-6)

The new I-270 bridge opened on September 2, 1966, and traffic fell to a trickle on the old bridge, which closed on February 29, 1970. The bridge was nearly torn down for scrap, and served as a set for the cheesy film *Escape from New York* **in 1981. In 1996, Gateway Trailnet leased the landmark and made it one of the longest bicycle and pedestrian bridges in the world. (1936, $12-15)**

The bluff overlooking the Chain of Rocks had been a beautifully landscaped recreation spot since the water works opened in 1894. By 1927, the Chain of Rocks Amusement Park had sprouted on the bluff. The Comet roller coaster shown here was torn down in 1958, the same year the park was renamed Chain of Rocks Fun Fair. (1946, $25-30)

Ike and Tina Turner, Paul Revere and the Raiders, and Tommy James and the Shondells played poolside events at Chain of Rocks before they became nationally famous. The park was doomed when Six Flags Over Mid-America opened at Eureka in 1971. Chain of Rocks Fun Fair closed forever on Labor Day, 1977. (1946, $20-25)

The Flexor Drive In Corporation opened the 66 Park In at 9438 Watson Road on September 26, 1947. The single screen drive-in could accommodate 800 cars. After less than half a season, the firm sold to Fred Wehrenberg. The wooded area across Highway 66 in this photo became Crestwood Plaza. Area across Watson Road in the photo below became Crestwood Plaza. *Courtesy Wehrenberg Archives (1948)*

The 66 Park In offered a Ferris wheel, a miniature train, and even trained bear cubs for the kids. The back of the screen facing Route 66 was lit up by miles of neon tubing, spelling out the name of the theatre. It closed after the 1993 season and was torn down in March 1994 to make room for a supermarket. *Courtesy Missouri State Archives (1958)*

The original ten Deco Moderne units of the Coral Court Motel were designed by Adolph Struebig for owner John Carr and opened in 1942. Another 23 units designed by Harold Tyrer were added in 1946. Three two-story frame buildings added in 1953 brought the total to 77 units, all nestled in a park-like setting. The attached garages and short-term rates later gave the Coral Court a racy reputation. (c. 1946, $25-30)

In September 1934, former bootleggers and brothers James and William Smith opened the Red Cedar Tavern in Pacific, built with red cedar logs. James Smith Jr. took over and hired Katherine Brinkman as a waitress. They married in 1940 and the business remained in the family until closing in March 2005. (c. 1946 $60-65)

In 1953, Carl Austin Hall and Bonnie Heady shocked the nation when they kidnapped and killed six-year-old Bobby Greenlease, son of a Kansas City millionaire. Hall holed up at the Coral Court with a prostitute before his arrest. Half of the $600,000 ransom was never found. The sign shown here was erected about that time. Sadly, the Coral Court was torn down in 1995 for construction of a subdivision. (c. 1955, $35-40)

"The World's Largest Roadside Restaurant" started as a simple structure dubbed the "Banana Stand," erected by Spencer Groff in 1924. This building at Route 66 and Missouri Route 100 opened on July 3, 1927, and was named after the shape of the lot. Louis Eckelcamp took over the Diamonds in 1935 and this building was destroyed by fire on February 25, 1948. (c. 1940 $15-20)

After the fire, the Diamonds operated out of a temporary structure until this deco building was ready in 1950. The name was painted in big letters on the roof, so even air travelers could spot the Diamonds. In 1967, the Diamonds moved to the interstate. This location became the Tri-County Truck Stop, but has been vacant since 2006. (1950, $12-15)

Dill claimed Jesse and Frank James used the cave as a hideout, dividing their ill-gotten gains at "Loot Rock." In 1949, Dill brought 102-year-old J. Frank Dalton to the cave, backing Dalton's claim that he was actually Jesse James and making front-page news. Dill gave the formations in the cave fanciful names, and is shown here pointing to "grapes in the Wine Room." (c. 1950, $4-6)

Lester Dill opened Meramec Caverns on Memorial Day 1933. With no time to build an entrance, he called it "the world's first drive in cave." Dill was a promotional genius, credited with inventing the bumper sticker. During the Cold War, ticket buyers also got a "Bomb Shelter Pass." Barns for hundreds of miles around were painted with ads for the cave. (c. 1938, $8-10)

Pauline Roberts and her husband Hallie took over the Wagon Wheel in 1963. Hallie died in 1980 and Pauline married Harold Armstrong in 1988. Along with caretaker Roy Mudd, they made the Wagon Wheel a Route 66 icon. They are all gone now, but Connie Echols took over the Wagon Wheel in 2009 and began renovations. (1951, $13-15)

The Wagon Wheel Motel in Cuba is among the best preserved classic Route 66 motels. It opened in 1934 as the Wagon Wheel Cabins, operated by Robert and Margaret Martin. In 1939, AAA declared that Wagon Wheel was "one of the best in the state." John and Winifred Pratt ran the motel from 1947 to 1963 (1946, $10-12)

Frank Ebling opened the Mule Trading Post west of Pacific in 1946. It was originally a restaurant as well as a gift shop, but Ebling decided to focus on the souvenir business. When I-44 bypassed Pacific in 1957, Ebling constructed a new trading post on the four-lane east of Rolla. (c. 1947, $60-65)

Billboards featuring the friendly mule were a familiar sight as far away as Joplin and the kids could ride a pair of real mules here in the 1970s. Herb Baden bought the Mule in 1966, selling to Jack and Janiece Wittman in 1995. Carl and Velma Smith run the Mule today and the neon mule on the sign still wiggles his ears. (1969, $4-6)

The Totem Pole has moved twice due to highway relocation. Harry and Edna Cochran opened the original near Arlington in 1933. Ralph and Catherine Jones bought the location on the new four-lane in 1957. The present incarnation of the Totem Pole on at Rolla opened in 1977. The original totem still stands inside. *Tim Jones* (c. 1935)

In 1957, Zeno Scheffer and his wife, Loretta, opened the 20-unit Zeno's Studio Motel where the new four-lane met the City Route west of Rolla. They added the steak house in 1959 and the motel was expanded to 32 units. Zeno's is still operated by the Scheffer family today, featuring 50 recently remodeled units. (1957, $5-7)

Jessie and Pete Hudson ran the Munger-Moss Sandwich Shop at Devil's Elbow, and moved the business to Lebanon after being bypassed. They added a motel next to their Munger Moss Restaurant in 1946. The Munger Moss originally had seven two-room structures, which were later enclosed and connected. *Courtesy of Ramona Lehmann* **(1946)**

Vernelle's Motel opened in 1938 as the Gasser Tourist Court. Fred and Vernelle Gasser bought it from their uncle in 1952 and Nye Goodridge took over in 1960. The restaurant was later relocated due to Route 66 expansion and then torn down for I-44 in 1968. Vernelle's was cut off by the I-44 realignment in 2005 but hangs on, run by Nye's son, Ed. (c. 1957, $4-6)

Time seems to have stood still in Devil's Elbow, where Old Route 66 twists and turns over steep grades. The road crosses a bridge built in 1923, offering views of the Big Piney River and spectacular bluffs. Dorothy and Atholl "Jiggs" Miller's Market opened in 1954. It became Allman's in 1982 and is now operated by Phillip Sheldon as Sheldon's Market. (1960, $3-5)

The famous Munger Moss sign was added along with the swimming pool in the 1950s. A sign marking the MODOT Route 66 Welcome Center on I-44 near Conway is a tribute to the one at the Munger Moss. Ramona and Bob Lehmann have operated the motel since 1971 and several rooms are decorated in Route 66 themes. (c. 1955, $4-6)

On January 21, 1930, the Colonel opened the Nelson Tavern. Despite the name, liquor was never served. The tavern was also surrounded by fantastic gardens, and the interior was filled with exotic plants. "Nelsonville" was torn down in 1958 after Interstate 44 was completed, and a supermarket stands here today. (c. 1931, $8-10)

Honorary Colonel Arthur Nelson worked hard to ensure that Missouri Route 14, later Route 66, came through Lebanon and donated right of way through his apple orchard. In 1926, Nelson opened a beautiful Conoco station, adding cabins amid lush gardens. The original eight cottages were named after the Route 66 states. (c. 1934, $6-8)

Colonel Nelson said the design for his tourist court came to him in a dream after he saw a musical fountain at the Chicago World's Fair in 1933. The 12 stone cabins of the "Dream Village" surrounded the fountain, where a light show was presented as music played. Nelson's Dream Village stayed in business until 1977. (c. 1936, $6-8)

Hillary and Mary Brightwell opened the Rest Haven Court at Springfield in 1947 and ran it until 1979. It originally had four cabins with eight units. Ten units were added in 1952. Ten more were added in 1955, and then all the units were enclosed. The gas station was later moved to the back of the complex and is used for storage. (1955, $13-15)

The Rest Haven is still in pristine condition. The sign was erected in 1953, and inspired the design of the sign at the Munger Moss Motel in Lebanon. The card advertises "100% Refrigerated Air-Conditioning – Steam Heat – Telephone – Beauty Rest Mattresses – Free Radio – Ice – Newspapers – Well Equipped Playground." (c. 1955, $4-6)

The Rail Haven Cottage Cabins opened in 1938 at Glenstone Avenue and St. Louis Street in Springfield. Lawrence Lippman, who built the court with his brother, is shown reading in one of the rooms on this brochure. The Rail Haven, "Look for the Rail Fence," advertised catering to "only the higher class tourists." (c. 1940, $15-20)

The tiny motor court grew into the Rail Haven Motel, 46 units on a beautiful three-acre lawn. "This nationally known motel is well furnished and equipped." Gordon Elliott revived the fading motel in 1994. It is now the nostalgic, yet thoroughly modern 93-unit Best Western Route 66 Rail Haven. (1957 $4-6)

Arthur Boots designed another Deco Moderne masterpiece for his drive-in restaurant across from the motel. The Boots Drive In was in operation from 1946 to 1970 and was operated by Arthur's son Bob Boots for many of those years. The altered but still recognizable building still stands today and houses a savings and loan. (1955, $60-65)

In 1939, Arthur Boots and Ida Boots opened their motel at the junction of U.S. 66 and U.S. 71 in Carthage. The rooms originally rented for $2.50 per night. Clark Gable once stayed in room number six. In 2003, The Boots was nearly torn down for a Walgreen's. But the deal fell apart amid an outcry from preservationists. (1957, $8-10)

Red and Julia Chaney opened their café in Springfield in 1947. Red ran out of room on the sign, so it became Red's Giant "Hamburg," home of the first drive up restaurant window. Red's was featured twice in *Rolling Stone* and immortalized in a rock song by the Morells. Red retired in 1984 and the building was leveled in 1999. *Courtesy Cathy Hickman and Tom Carter, Ozarks Public Television* (c. 1982)

Original 66 through St. Louis • 1926-1932

The official 1926 Missouri state map shows Route 66 from the McKinley Bridge using 9th Street, Salisbury Street, Natural Bridge Avenue, Grand Blvd., Delmar Blvd., Sarah Street, Lindell Blvd., Skinker Blvd., and McCausland Avenue to Manchester Road. (AAA placed the signs, so all the U.S. highways passing through St. Louis at the time were routed past AAA headquarters on Lindell.)

A year later, 66 drivers were following the same route to Lindell, and then turning onto Boyle Avenue, following Clayton Avenue through Forest Park and Dogtown, and McCausland to Manchester. In 1929, the route was moved to the Municipal (MacArthur) Bridge and then followed 7th Street to Chouteau Avenue, Boyle, Clayton, and McCausland to Manchester. The McKinley Bridge route was then marked as "Optional 66" with a few variations until 1937.

Route 66 originally crossed the Mississippi River on the McKinley Bridge, named after Congressman William B. McKinley. He owned the interurban electric railway that constructed the bridge. Railroad traffic ran down the center, with vehicle traffic on the outside of the superstructure. Today, the outside lanes are for bicycles and pedestrians. (c. 1910 $20-25)

This view of St. Louis shows the 37 square blocks cleared for the Jefferson National Expansion Memorial beginning in 1939. The barren wasteland was used as a parking lot for two decades, due to two wars, and haggling over who would pay to relocate the railroad tracks on the riverfront. Work resumed in 1959. *Missouri State Archives* **(1955)**

Eero Saarinen won a 1947 competition to design the Jefferson National Expansion Memorial with his vision of a 630-foot tall arch covered in stainless steel. The last section was lifted into place on October 28, 1965. The Gateway Arch is our nation's tallest national monument. Saarinen didn't live to see it completed. He died in 1961. (1965)

The Old Cathedral was constructed in 1834. It is the oldest Catholic cathedral west of the Mississippi and the only building left when the riverfront was cleared for the Jefferson National Expansion Memorial. The 3rd Street Expressway (Route 66) is at the left in this view, where Memorial Drive and the depressed lanes of I-70 are today. *Missouri State Archives* (1964)

Slaves were once sold on the steps of the Old Courthouse, where the first trials in the Dred Scott case took place beginning in 1847. Scott was a slave who sued for freedom after his owner took him to a free state. The U.S. Supreme Court ruled that slaves were not citizens, and therefore could not sue. (c. 1956, $1-2)

The Cardinals played at Sportsman's Park from 1892 to 1898 and moved back in 1920. It was also the home of the Browns from 1902 until they moved to Baltimore in 1953. Also in 1953, Anheuser-Busch took over and changed the name to Busch Stadium. The Cardinals played the final game at Grand Avenue and Dodier Street on May 8, 1966, and the site is now the Herbert Hoover Boys and Girls Club. (c. 1960, $8-10)

The first game at Busch Memorial Stadium downtown took place on May 12, 1966. Busch hosted the 1966 All-Star Game and the World Series in 1967, 1968, 1982, 1985, 1987, and 2004. It was also the home of the NFL Cardinals, and the Rams played here in 1995. It was demolished in 2005. (1966, $2-4)

The Hotel Jefferson on 12th Street (now Tucker) opened on May 1, 1904, just in time to house guests headed to the World's Fair. It originally had 350 rooms, expanded to 800 in 1927. The last guest checked out on February 25, 1975. It most recently provided housing for seniors, but has since closed. (c. 1945, $3-5)

Looking east on Market Street towards 12th Street (now Tucker), the Civil Courts Building is at left. It replaced the Old Courthouse in June 1930. The top is a replica of the Tomb of Mausolus at Halicarnassus in present day Turkey, one of the Seven Wonders of the Ancient World. Kiel Auditorium is at right. *Missouri State Archives* (1955)

The Soldier's Memorial at the left was dedicated in 1936. The Missouri Pacific Building behind it was designed with 35 floors, but the Great Depression halted construction at 23. The 28-story Southwestern Bell Building at right opened in 1929. It has 17 step backs to minimize shadows on the surrounding streets. (1950s, $2-4)

The Municipal Auditorium opened on April 14, 1934, and was attached to the opera house fronting on Market Street. It was built by Mayor Henry Kiel's construction firm, and named in his honor in 1942. The auditorium was demolished for the new Kiel Center, now the Scott Trade Center, in 1991. The Opera House is currently being redeveloped. (1943, $2-4)

Union Station opened on September 1, 1894. Over 100,000 passengers per day passed through during World War II. The station fell on hard times after the last passenger train departed on October 31, 1978. But it reopened as a shopping destination and hotel complex on August 29, 1985. *Missouri State Archives* **(1955)**

The design of the St. Louis City Hall is patterned after the Hotel de Ville, or City Hall, in Paris. Construction began on July 18, 1890, and was not completed until November 5, 1904, because no bonds were issued for construction. The central tower and two smaller towers shown here were removed in 1936. (1930s, $1-3)

Preston Bradshaw's Coronado Hotel at Lindell Boulevard and Spring Avenue opened in 1925 and hosted notables such as Charles Lindbergh, Rudolph Valentino, and Harry Truman. It became a college dormitory after closing in 1964. In 2003, the restored Coronado reopened as a restaurant, residential and office complex. (c. 1950, $1-3)

Purina Mills founder William Danforth used a checkerboard to illustrate his belief in balancing our physical, social, mental, and religious lives. In 1902, the animal feed maker joined with Webster Edgerly, cereal maker and founder of the Ralstonism health movement. Ralston-Purina headquarters became famous as Checkerboard Square. The firm merged with a subsidiary of Nestle in 2001. (c. 1955, $13-15)

Work began on the New Cathedral at Lindell Boulevard and Newstead Avenue on May 1, 1907, and it was consecrated on June 29, 1926. Completion of the mosaics was not finished until 1988. Pope John the Second designated it as the Cathedral Basilica of St. Louis in 1997 and visited during his historic trip to St. Louis in October 1999. (c. 1932, $1-3)

The Chase Park Plaza has hosted royalty, presidents, and entertainment legends. Chase Ullman opened his hotel in 1922. Sam Koplar began work on the Park Plaza next door in 1929 and took over the Chase in 1946. They were combined in 1961. The Chase closed in 1989, but was restored and reopened in 1999. (1950s, $1-3)

From 1927-1933, Route 66 cut through southern Forest Park, which is 450 acres larger than Central Park in New York. It opened on June 24, 1876, and hosted 20 million visitors during the 1904 World's Fair. The Barnes Hospital towers on Kingshighway are visible in the background. Note the shields for U.S. 66 and U.S. 50 at the lower right. (c. 1932, $55-60) *Missouri Department of Transportation*

The Forest Park Highlands, just east of Route 66 on Oakland Avenue, began as a simple beer garden in 1896 and grew into the premiere amusement park in the city. Most of the amusement park was destroyed by fire on July 19, 1963. The site is now Forest Park Community College. (c. 1915, $8-10)

The first St. Louis Zoo was located in Fairgrounds Park. A small collection of animals came to Forest Park in 1891. The addition of the giant bird-cage from the Smithsonian display at the 1904 World's Fair spurred more development. It is now one of the most renowned zoos in the nation and admission is free. (c. 1932, $1-3)

The Arena opened in 1929. It was built to house the National Dairy Show, but the Great Depression bankrupted the promoters. The "Old Barn" was the home of the NHL St. Louis Blues from 1967-1994 and hosted countless events and concerts. It was imploded on February 27, 1999, for a suburban style office park. (c. 1930, $15-20)

The Hi Pointe Standard sign used as much current as a town of 1,000. It was 40 feet wide and 70 feet to the top with 5,800 lamps, 2,900 feet of neon tubing, and five miles of wire. It was replaced with an equally large Plexiglas sign in 1961, changed to read "Amoco" in 1985. L.C. Stephenson ran the station from 1933 until 1985. (1930s, $95-100)

William Medart's luncheonette in a log cabin on Clayton Avenue developed into an early drive-in and kept growing. Medart's would become the Rose and Crown before Stephen Apted took over in 1963 and turned it into the Cheshire Inn. In 2009, it was transformed into a Swiss Chalet for the film ***Up in the Air*****, starring George Clooney. (1950s, $8-10)**

Original Route 66 followed Manchester through Maplewood. When James Sutton died in 1877, he left his land to be divided among his nine children. One daughter, Mary C. Marshall, sold to St. Louis real estate men. They laid out a subdivision, planted maple trees along the streets, and called it Maplewood. The city was incorporated in 1908.
Courtesy of Missouri State Archives

Isaac and Michael Katz founded their chain of stores in Kansas City. St. Louis locations included one at Highway 66 and Elm, on Kirkwood Road, and this one on Manchester in Maplewood. The stores were known for catchy advertising slogans and low prices. Katz was sold to Skaggs in 1970, and Skaggs became Osco in 1984. (c. 1950s, $15-20)

Buckingham's Restaurant advertised "Table d'Hote," or family style dinners, "where polite people assemble." It was originally a private residence, converted to a restaurant in the 1920s. This building still stands on the north side of Manchester Road west of Annalee Avenue. (c. 1946, $6-8)

Henry Bartold and his brother Frederick built this inn and tavern on Manchester Road at Deer Creek in 1849. Bartold's Grove had a picnic ground on the hill behind the building, which was also a stagecoach stop and housed the first post office in the area. The Sunnen Industrial Complex occupies this site today. *Library of Congress* **(1936)**

The Pierce-Pennant Oil Company built the Big Chief in 1929. The restaurant, gas station, and 62 cabins with attached garages surrounded a beautiful courtyard. Manager Si Hensien said every guest "got a square deal, very well fed, and what they want to drink." The main building remains and is now the Big Chief Roadhouse. (1929, $25-30)

Manchester was originally known as Hoardstown, after settler Jesse Hoard. In 1825, it was named after another settler's hometown in England. After Route 66 shifted south, Manchester became U.S. 50 and then Missouri Route 100. Today, Manchester is clogged with traffic and lined with retail businesses. *Courtesy of Margie Stout* (1929, $65-70)

The Manchester Drive In was the first in the St. Louis area, opening in 1940 on a 50-acre site. It became prime real estate after the completion of I-244 (now I-270) in 1965 and was torn down in 1967 to make room for West County Center. The shopping center with its landmark sign featuring a stylized dove opened in February 1969. *City of Des Peres* (1940s)

Historic Route 66 • 1933-1975

The Historic or Southern Route may be the most famous because of landmarks such as Ted Drewes Frozen Custard and the late 66 Park In and Coral Court, but it was not the main line of Route 66 during the glory years.

On August 5-6, 1933, the New Watson Road in St. Louis and Franklin Counties opened to traffic and Manchester lost its U.S. 66 designation. The main route from the Municipal Bridge then basically followed 7th Street, Chouteau Avenue, 12th Street, Gravois Avenue, Chippewa Street, Watson Road, and then passed through Pacific. The route from the McKinley Bridge became "Optional 66" or "City 66."

The MAINLINE of Route 66 was moved to the Chain of Rocks Bridge and Lindbergh Blvd. in 1936. The route over the Municipal Bridge and Watson was then designated as "City 66." Another "City 66" was established to mostly follow Riverview Drive, Broadway, Calvary Avenue, Florissant Avenue, Warne Avenue, Carter Avenue, back to Florissant Avenue, and then jogging onto 12th Street (now Tucker). Those alignments were basically in effect until 1955, when the route began shifting again due to freeway construction.

The Municipal Bridge carried Route 66 from 1929 to 1935 and "City 66" from 1936 to 1955. It was named for General Douglas MacArthur in 1942 and closed to vehicles in 1981.The *S.S. Admiral* offered excursions from 1940 until 1979, and was the largest river cruise ship in the world. The once proud ship, stripped of her engines and lavish interior, became a casino that struggled and closed in 2010.
Missouri State Archives **(1953)**

August A. Busch Sr. built the Bevo Mill in 1916 halfway between the brewery and his Grant's Farm home, just south of where Route 66 turns from Gravois Avenue to Chippewa Street. The Mill Room was his private dining room and Busch opened the restaurant to the public in 1917. The brewery gave the landmark to the City of St. Louis in 2009. (c. 1925, $8-10)

The Donut Drive-In at 6526 Chippewa Street opened in 1952. There was no drive-up window. "Drive-In" simply meant off street parking was available. With help from a National Park Service Route 66 Corridor Preservation Grant, the sign with its animated dropping red neon donuts was restored in 2008. *Courtesy John, Paul, Jim and Chuck Schwarz* **(1970s)**

Charlie Mittino's Shangri-La, "The Club Beautiful," was located in the 6600 block of Watson Road and opened in 1940. In 1946, they advertised a "Deluxe Century Steak Dinner" for $2.75 and touted Grace Niggli performing on the organ. "We specialize in Fine Foods." Garavelli's Restaurant occupies this building today. (1946, $10-12)

Route 66 in South St. Louis was a major shopping destination. The Southtown Famous Barr department store was located at Kingshighway and Chippewa Street from 1951 to 1994. This view shows the Hampton Village Shopping Center, at Chippewa and Hampton. The first shopping center in St. Louis started out as a farmer's market in 1939. *Missouri State Archives*

The Wayside Motel opened in 1940, across from the Coral Court. It is still in business today, although the classic neon sign, with its blinking colored bubbles, has been replaced. The Duplex Motel (opened in 1936) and the Chippewa Motel (opened in 1938) are still standing nearby. (c. 1946, $8-10)

The Missouri Motel opened in 1950 at 8084 Watson Road with a design obviously influenced by the Coral Court. It advertised "Hot Water Heat – Television, Air-Conditioned." Like the Coral Court, each unit also had an attached garage. The motel was torn down in the 1970s. *Missouri State Archives* (1955)

La Casa Grande Motel, 8208 Watson Road, advertised "Like a Fine Motel," offering "Steam heated cottages with tile showers – Terrazzo floors and radios. Individual garage with each cottage." It still stands, although the neon sign is gone. The motel's Pueblo Revival style architecture is usually found in the Southwest. (c. 1947, $55-60)

The 66 Auto Court at 8730 Watson Road was billed as "St. Louis' Finest Modern Auto Court." The advertisements asked "Why Spend the Night in the City?" and noted that the 66 was only 15 minutes from downtown St. Louis with insulated rooms and innerspring mattresses. The site is now the Watson Auto Care Plaza. (1946, $12-15)

This couple, Lynn and Don Hubatka, is posed at the Evergreen Cabins, 8723 Watson Road. Otto Mayer opened the 14 cabins in the early 1940s. Allie and Alvena Langbein took over in 1948 and Emil Wildermuth owned them from 1960 until they were torn down in 1968. The Evergreen Apartments were built on the site. *Courtesy of William and Susan Dempster* (1965)

Each unit at the Motel Royal, "Traveler's Paradise," had an attached garage and opened to a landscaped private parkway and beautiful, expansive grounds. The motel at 9282 Watson Road was completed in 1951. An office building occupies this site today. (1951, $6-8)

The Oaks Motel and Package Liquor Store was at 9285 Watson Road, where Montgomery Bank stands today. From the back of the card, "16 rooms with private tile bath in each room – hot and cold water – porter and maid service – Beauty Rest mattresses." (c. 1950, $15-20)

The Blue Haven Motel at 10000 Watson Road began as a private residence and grew to 24 units, owned by Sol Schlansky from 1955 to 1975. A medical office building stands on the site at 10000 Watson Road today. The card advertises "24 units. Air-cooled. Gas Heat, Some kitchenettes. Spacious grounds and playground." (c. 1955, $15-20)

The Blue Bonnet Court with its 18 tidy brick cottages opened in 1938 at 10100 Watson Road. The card described the Blue Bonnet as "Safe – Quiet – Refined – Modern fireproof insulated brick cottages and city water." The court advertised for "Tourists Only." Johnny Mac's Sporting Goods is now located here. (1946, $8-10)

Offering "Ultra modern tourist cottages," a coffee shop, dining room, and lounge, the Twin Six Court at 10230 Watson Road was constructed by the Sinwell Brothers in 1940. It was later owned by A.W. Aschinger and was torn down in 1986. A bank stands on this site today. (c. 1955, $6-8)

On August 20, 1931, the first cloverleaf interchange west of the Mississippi opened at Watson Road and Lindbergh Boulevard (at that time, State Highway 77). In 1936, it became the junction of U.S. 66 (Lindbergh) and City 66. (Watson) The overpass trimmed with pink granite was replaced in 1980. *Missouri Department of Transportation* (1965)

The Sunset Ranch Motel opened in 1952 on the south side of Route 66 near Weiss Airport. Airport owner Gene Taylor also ran the motel. According to Norma Maret Bolin in *The Route 66 St. Louis Cookbook,* airport owner Gener Taylor also ran the motel. The Rose Lawn and the Siesta Motels were also located along this stretch on the south side of the highway. (1955, $13-15)

Looking north on Lindbergh from Watson, the Park Plaza Motel is at left and Steak n' Shake is just to the north. Other Steak n' Shake locations on 66 included Watson at Elm Avenue, Watson at Sappington Road, Chippewa Street at Morganford Road, and the area's first, opened on December 4, 1948, at 6622 Chippewa. *Missouri State Archives* (1955)

Weiss Airport was originally a grass landing strip on farmland owned by brothers Wilburn and Harley Weiss along with Harley's wife, Ruth. Route 66 was just 60 feet north of the runway. The airport was in operation until 1994. An office park and the Fairfield Inn occupy the site today. *Courtesy of Margie Stout* (c. 1957, $15-20)

The southeast corner of Route 66 and Missouri Route 141 was known as Kessler's Corner, after this restaurant and tavern specializing in "chicken and frog dinners." In 1935, the area was incorporated as Peerless Park, a community of about 50 people best known for fireworks stands. Peerless Park was disincorporated in 1999. (c. 1940, $15-20)

The Wuenhmueller family opened Sylvan Beach Park in the early 1930s at a rare spot on the Meramec River where it was fairly safe to swim. Most of it was wiped out for construction of the I-44 bridges, although the pool did survive awhile longer. The site is now part of Emmenegger Nature Park. (c. 1951, $15-20)

Halinar's Cabins were among the closest to St. Louis to use a construction style typical to the Ozarks region. Many roadside businesses were covered in sandstone slabs called "Giraffe Rock." Halinar's also included a frame gas station and café. The site is now part of the 180-acre Maritz Incorporated headquarters complex. (c. 1946, $35-40)

Lyle and Ruby Overman built the 16 cottages of the Trav-O-Tel Court in 1933, on the New Route 66 at Old Antire Road. They sold to Mr. and Mrs. A. Ott in 1940. The Overmans moved to Oklahoma City, where they operated the Major and Carlyle Motels on Route 66. This site flooded frequently, and the Trav-O-Tel is long gone. (c. 1945, $25-30)

Times Beach on the Meramec River was founded as a promotion by the *St. Louis Times* newspaper in 1925. Waste oil was sprayed on the dusty streets in the 1970s. After a disastrous flood in 1982, residents learned the oil was contaminated with dioxin. The town was leveled and the decontaminated site is now Route 66 State Park. *Missouri Department of Transportation* (1925)

The Bridgehead Inn opened in 1935 and became a haven for gambling and other illicit activities. Edward Steinberg took over in 1947, cleaned things up, and ran Steiny's here until 1972. The restaurant was later known as the Galley West, and served as the EPA headquarters during the cleanup of Times Beach. It now houses the Route 66 State Park visitor's center. (1940, $30-35)

Deke Keeton built the Rock City Café, cabins, and gas station between the Frisco and Missouri Pacific tracks. Ed LaMar's Ozark Café and tourist court, tavern, and gas station were immediately to the east. The buildings were similar, so both businesses became known as Rock City. It was all torn down for I-44 in 1955. (c. 1940, $35-40)

Fred and Jean Miller opened the Al-Pac Restaurant in 1942, naming it for the communities of Allenton and Pacific. The restaurant portion, with its cedar dining room, became a lounge and burned down in 1976, but part of the lodge and motel they added on later still stands. (c. 1946, $35-40)

Former major league baseball player Bob Klinger owned a gas station just east of Central Avenue in Eureka and rented the log restaurant building to Lou Gerwe. Gerwe's later became Don and Dot Hanephin's Log House Café. It was torn down after the Hanephins relocated in 1959. Eureka High School is in the background. (c. 1946, $35-40)

The Beacon Court opened in 1946 with "14 Modern, Inviting, Tastefully Decorated Cottages." The owners placed a beacon atop an old windmill derrick converted into a sign. The motel closed in the early 1980s, but George and Monica Mahler restored the sign and placed it at their Beacon Car Wash. (1960, $3-5)

The sandstone bluffs of the Meramec River line the north side of Route 66 entering Pacific. Since the 1870s, the bluffs have been mined for silica sand used in fine glassware. The bluffs were cut back when the new highway was constructed in 1932, exposing these "caves" created by the miners. (c. 1940, $2-4)

Mainline and Bypass Route 66 1936-1965

Route 66 was routed across the Chain of Rocks Bridge in 1936. It followed today's Dunn Road and Lindbergh through Kirkwood to meet the Watson Road "City 66." The Chain of Rocks route became "Bypass 66" in 1955 when the mainline moved to the Veteran's (now King) Bridge to take advantage of new expressways in Metro East and the Third Street Expressway in downtown St. Louis. The mainline then continued out Gravois and Chippewa to Watson. The "Bypass 66" signs moved to the newly completed segment of I-270 between Lindbergh and Riverview Drive in 1963 and came down in 1965.

The Knotty Pine Motel was located at what is now Dunn Road and Taylor Road in Hazelwood, where Apache Village R.V. Center is today. There was also a motel named the Knotty Pine at Lindbergh and Olive Street Road that survived into the 1980s. It was located across from the Ivy Motel, which still stands. (c. 1950, $40-45)

The Parrett Brothers, Jim, Bill, Tom, and their families, made Parrett's Restaurant a well-known stop for chicken and steak dinners at Route 66 and 5th Street in Pacific. The restaurant was in operation from 1932 to 1974. The building was demolished and a dentist office is located here today. (c. 1945, $45-50)

Henry Ford's grandson, Benson Ford, dedicated the St. Louis Assembly Plant on Route 66 near Robertson (now Hazelwood) in September 1948. It covered three million square feet under one roof, producing Mercury and Ford automobiles until 1984. It later produced the Aerostar minivan and Ford Explorer before closing in 2006. The plant was demolished for an industrial and office development. (1966, $4-6)

Lambert International Airport was originally a balloon launch site named Kinloch Field, where Teddy Roosevelt became the first president to fly in an airplane. Charles Lindbergh flew the mail from here. Albert Bond Lambert developed the field at his own expense and sold it to the city for the price he paid for the land alone in 1928. *Missouri State Archives* **(1955)**

McDonnell Aircraft built the *Mercury* **and** *Gemini* **space capsules and military jets like the** *Banshee*, *Demon,* **and** *Voodoo.* **McDonnell merged with Douglas Aircraft in 1967 and up to 40,000 people worked here at one time. F4** *Phantom II* **fighters are shown here outside the final assembly building. McDonnell-Douglas merged with Boeing in 1996.** *McDonnell-Douglas photo* **(1971)**

The first Lambert Field terminal was built in 1933. The "Union Station of the Air" could handle four planes at once, criticized at the time as too large. The *Condor* **shown here was the first one built at the Curtiss-Wright Lambert Field factory. The present terminal opened in 1956 and this structure was torn down in 1979.** *Courtesy of Margie Stout* **(1933, $35-40)**

The Motel St. Louis opened in 1953 at 5028 North Lindbergh and stood until the airport expanded in the late 1960s. "When you travel, you'll be proud to say – I stopped at the new Motel St. Louis." The card advertised "Ultra-modern rooms – Air conditioned for your comfort – Television for your pleasure." (c. 1955, $8-10)

In 1951, Frank and Edna Bulan opened a motel next to their home across from Lambert Airport. The back of the card touts "10 brick units with tile shower, Beautyrest beds, radio in every room." Bulan's grew to 17 units before being torn down about the same time as the Motel St. Louis. (c. 1955, $8-10)

Stanley and Olivia Williams opened their "Cour-Tel" on the southwest side of Lindbergh at Natural Bridge in 1950 and ran it until 1976. The Apollo I astronauts stayed here while visiting McDonnell Aircraft. The Stanley was in business until 2001, when it was demolished for a controversial new airport runway. (c. 1955, $8-10)

The Air-O-Way Courts at 4125 North Lindbergh were owned by Mr. and Mrs. Michael Rampani and opened in 1948, offering "16 new, steamheated Permastone Cottages." Harold Jones changed the name to the Air Way in the 1970s. It was demolished in 1998 for construction of a Home Depot. (c. 1950, $10-12)

The Sunset Acres Motel opened at 3720 North Lindbergh in 1950 and was owned by Mr. and Mrs. Frank J. Lama. They advertised "Ultra-modern accommodations. Airfoam mattresses and pillows, Mengel Furniture." It was demolished for the construction of Northwest Plaza Shopping Center in 1964. (c. 1960, $6-8)

The Smith Brothers Motel opened in 1943. Lester Neiman and Alvin Block took over in 1945 and named it the King Brothers Motel. It grew to a complex that could accommodate over 600 guests. In 1974, Developer Donald Breckenridge incorporated parts of it into his Breckenridge Inn, now the Hilton St. Louis Frontenac. (1955, $13-15)

The Kirkwood City Hall was built in 1941. On February 7, 2008, a disgruntled resident went on a shooting spree here, killing policemen William Biggs and Tom Ballman, council members Connie Karr and Michael Lynch, and Public Works Director Ken Yost. Mayor Mike Swoboda died from his wounds on September 6.

Lindbergh Boulevard is renamed Kirkwood Road between Manchester and I-44. Kirkwood retains a small town atmosphere with landmarks such as Spencer's Grill, where the exterior is little changed since 1947. Trains still bring traffic to a halt and a neon sign directs motorists to a railroad overpass one block to the west. *Courtesy of Margie Stout* (c. 1945, $30-35)

Architect Bernard McMahon built the Westward Motel in 1953 on the northeast corner of Watson and Lindbergh. McMahon went on to construct more hotels, as well as the Sevens Building in Clayton. A Hampton Inn stands on the Westward site today and the sign can be seen at the Museum of Transportation on Barrett Station Road. (1957, $6-8)

The first planned suburb west of the Mississippi was named for James Pugh Kirkwood, the chief engineer of the Pacific Railroad. The Missouri Pacific Depot was constructed in 1893. Concerned residents prevented the structure from being "modernized" in 1941 and Amtrak trains still stop here today. *Courtesy of Margie Stout* (c. 1948, $25-30)

The Park Plaza Courts (later the Ozark Plaza Motel) and Nelson's Café were on the northwest side of the Lindbergh and Watson interchange, where the route via the Chain of Rocks Bridge met the southern route through St. Louis. The Holiday Inn Southwest-Viking Conference Center occupies the site today. (1955, $10-12)

The Meramec Valley

After crossing into Franklin County, Route 66 runs atop a ridge and then descends into the valley of the Bourbeuse River. It then follows the plateau between the Bourbeuse and the Meramec River Valleys. The highway for miles around is dotted with billboards and the occasional barn emblazoned with advertisements for one of the most famous roadside attractions on Route 66, Meramec Caverns at Stanton. The Route 66 traveler then passed through St. Clair, originally known as Traveler's Repose until the townsfolk got tired of being mistaken for a cemetery. Sullivan is next, founded by Stephen and Dorcas Sullivan in 1856.

Route 66 between St. Louis and the Missouri Botanical Garden Arboretum (now the Shaw Nature Preserve) was decorated with thousands of trees and flowers. In 1937, it was named the Henry Shaw Gardenway in honor of the founder of the Missouri Botanical Garden. Louis Eckelcamp built the Gardenway Motel in 1945. (c. 1955, $3-5)

Ed and Dell Moore ran the Crest Restaurant and cabins, located where M & M Sales is today, west of Pacific. "We Specialize in Chicken and Steak Dinners." The restaurant was classy enough to accept reservations. The station is selling Texaco gas in this view, but later sold D-X products. (c. 1940s, $35-40)

Jim Dailey was the original owner of the Cave Café and a motel next door. The motel building, later used as housing for café employees, no longer stands. The café building later became a gas station and now houses Kim Pogue's Good Heart Enterprises. (c. 1946, $30-35)

The American Inn opened about 1930. The restaurant, famous for Sunday chicken dinners, was located on the first floor of the log building. The owners lived upstairs. Mary Ellen Knight turned the gas station building into a day care center, operating it from 1973 to 2005. It became the Love and Learn Child Care Center. (c. 1946, $13-15)

In 1946, the Lovelace family constructed the Sunset Motel. Oliver Lee and Loleta Krueger ran the Sunset from 1971 to 2006. It is now operated by her daughter Connie and Connie's husband, Herman Grimes. The sign was restored in 2009 with assistance from the Route 66 Association of Missouri and a grant from the Route 66 Corridor Preservation Program. (c. 1950, $13-15)

The Pin Oak Motel took its name from the Pin Oak trees that surround it and nearby Pin Oak Creek. The eight-unit motel was constructed about 1940 by the Lovelace family, who later built the Sunset Motel. George Sweeney owned the motel when the Interstate arrived and killed the business. The Pin Oak was later converted to storage units. (c. 1955, $6-8)

The St. Clair Motel advertised "Ultra Modern Rooms. Radio-TV-Air Cond. – Electric Heating – Tubs – Showers." It was constructed in the early 1940s. Owners have included Mr. and Mrs. Pete Krifka, Fred and Mary Leen, Faye Hermling, as well as Walter and Kitty Crumbaker. The motel is still in business today. (c. 1950, $12-15)

This view looks west at the Twin Bridges over the Bourbeuse (burr-bus) River. The original seven-panel Pratt through truss bridge opened in 1925 and its twin was added to carry eastbound traffic in 1935. A sign on the approach warned "Caution – Careful Driving Required." They were replaced when I-44 was constructed. (1941, $2-4)

The Hilltop Café was operated by Max and Laverta Pracht near Hilltop Road where Route 66 descends into Bourbeuse River Valley. There were no tables, just 23 stools at the counter. A T-bone steak dinner for $1.65 was the most expensive item on the menu. The Hilltop closed after the arrival of I-44 and no longer stands. (c. 1950, $40-45)

Charlie Johnson and his son Robert operated Johnson's Motel in St. Clair. They would move to the new four-lane highway in 1952 to open the Skylark Motel. This building still stands, occupied by a realtor. The Skylark also remains, notable for its pillar with glass block inserts. The Skylark now houses the VFW Hall. (c. 1955, $35-40)

In 1938, Virgil Lewis established his café with seven stools and seven booths and offering "ho-made" pie. The café expanded next door in 1966. Virgil's nephew, Fred Short, and his wife, Marie, ran it from 1973 to 1995, when their son Chris took over. The Lewis Café is still a landmark, known for its fine beef raised at the family farm. (c. 1948, $25-30)

Lewis' Cafe,
St. Clair, Mo.

Twenty years faithful service. Home cooked meals, ho-made pie, humidor fresh cigars, photo finishing, films, cameras and supplies.
SERVING GOOD COFFEE - 5 ¢

Arch Bart built the Sunset Inn in the late 1920s. It later became Scully's Restaurant. Scully was once a chef at the famous Busch's Grove outside St. Louis. This building was torn down for construction of the four-lane in 1952. Scully's moved to the service road, and that structure is now occupied by Agape House. (c. 1940, $45-50)

Leslie and Margie Hilliard ran the Hilliard Rock Village Restaurant and motel. Margie displayed her doll collection inside, and then began importing dolls and selling them to collectors. Some of them were very expensive. The business closed in 1977 and the doll collection was auctioned off after Margie died in April 1988. (c. 1946, $55-60)

The Ozark Café was part of a complex owned by a retired St. Louis police officer who levied fines as a justice of the peace, making this part of Route 66 a notorious speed trap. The motel had a distinctive sign featuring a deer, which stood for years after the place closed. Only a small portion of the motel stands today. (c. 1950, $55-60)

The New England Pantry was originally a private home. Mrs. Conant, who had moved to the Ozarks from New England, operated it. The restaurant naturally became known for clam chowder. The Cape Cod cottage styled building still stands today and is a private home once again. (c. 1946, $50-55)

The Motel Meramec was originally a private home that faced the railroad tracks. It was turned around when Route 66 was constructed and later developed into Kovac's Restaurant and Motel, "Where Chicken and Dumplings are Dee-Licious." The building is once again a private residence. (c. 1955, $8-10)

Mr. and Mrs. Lewis J. Benson opened their Tourist City in 1937. It included a 24-hour café, gas station, and 16 "all approved AAA cabins." The complex became the McGinnis Show Me Courts when Mr. and Mrs. R.E. McGinnis took over. It also was later known as the Del Crest. Part of the complex still stands. (c. 1955, $12-15)

STANTON MOTEL
Located on Highway 66 at Stanton, Mo.

Advertised as the "Nearest Motel to Meramec Caverns," the Stanton Motel still caters to Route 66 travelers today and has a vintage neon sign out front. The back of the card advertised that the motel was "Air Conditioned," with "Central Heat, tubs and showers, low rates." (c. 1950, $6-8)

Edgar and Olive Randleman owned this cafe and garage just west of Stanton. In 1939, Edgar helped catch three escaped prisoners from Iowa when he tipped the State Patrol that three suspicious characters had stopped at the café. The men were captured near Eureka. (1941, $55-60)

Preston Pryser's Martha Jane Farm Auto Court Deluxe was one of the first between St. Louis and Springfield to have hot and cold water, showers, and toilets in each cottage. Ed and Edna Wagner took over in 1946. The family later changed the name to Pine Acres Motel and closed it down in 1970. The home and some cabins still stand. (c. 1940, $45-50)

This card described the Sunrise Motel, "66 miles west of St. Louis on new Highway 66," as a "Modern Motel" with "Big, airy, quiet homelike cabins, each with modern tile bath." Later views show the motel painted pink. It was demolished in 2007 to make way for a new overpass. (c. 1955, $15-20)

The Grande Courts advertised, "All strictly modern cottages with free garages" and a service station open 24 hours. The complex was extensively remodeled and expanded about 1958 and advertised as "The Pride of Sullivan." It was later known as the Hitching Post and then became the Family Motor Inn. (1957, $13-15)

Mr. and Mrs. Fred Snell Sr. opened their café in 1949. "Awful Good Food" was their slogan. When the neighboring Grande Courts became the Hitching Post, the restaurant also took the name and advertised, "Pipin' Hot Biscuits and Apple Butter." The building later became an antique mall, but now appears to be vacant. (1957, $3-5)

A private home was converted into the Sullmo Hotel and Cabins about 1935. Owner Charles Albrecht said, "You have tried the rest now try the best." The card advertised "Running water in each cabin, hot and cold showers," as well as "Drinking water as pure as a lily. Approved by the State Board of Health." (c. 1935, $10-12)

The Shamrock Motel was built for F.E. Dobbs in 1945 and has some of the most beautiful rock work on any motel in the Ozarks. The work was done by Grandpa Berti, an Italian stonemason. John and Rose Weiland took over in 1953. The building is still owned by the family and currently used as apartments. (c. 1955, $8-10)

Leasburg to Rolla

At Leasburg, there's another opportunity for the 66 traveler to see an underground marvel at Onondaga Caverns. Route 66 then heads into Bourbon, and past the water towers that are a favorite for photographers. The name came from railroad workers buying bourbon at the local store. Cuba is known as "Mural City USA" for the fine murals on buildings illustrating the history of the town. The highway crosses the wine-producing region around Rosati and heads through St. James.

Rolla is the home of the Missouri University of Science and Technology, formerly the University of Missouri-Rolla. One of the town founders wanted to name the community after his hometown of Raleigh, North Carolina. Everyone agreed and the name was spelled the way he pronounced it, "Rolla."

This group is exploring Mammothe Cave, opened to the public as Onondaga in 1904. The name is Iroquois for "Spirit of the Mountain." From 1932 until World War II one owner called his side Missouri Caverns and his rival touted Onondaga. Lester Dill of Meramec Caverns took over both in 1953 and made Onondaga Cave nationally famous. *James Memorial Library* **(c. 1900)**

The Bourbon Lodge was opened in 1932 by Alex and Edith Mortenson. The cabins with no plumbing rented for 50 cents per night and a sign out front advertised "Cooked Food." The lodge is now a private home, and the cabins are in ruins. The Mortensons moved a bit west in the early 1940s and built the High Hill Tourist Camp. (c. 1939, $35-40)

The White Swan Restaurant and Standard Station in Sullivan also served as the Greyhound Bus Stop. Dale McCanless and his wife, Barb, operated the White Swan at one time and also were owners of the Skylark Restaurant and Motel in St. Clair. The building was demolished in 1989 and Strauser Drugs is located here now. (c. 1946, $35-40)

The Red Horse Cabins were operated by Mr. and Mrs. C.C. Cox. The Red Horse became a truck stop billed as, "The largest between St. Louis and Springfield" before a 1953 fire destroyed the café/station and closed down Route 66 for a time. Some of the cabins and the home still stand. (c. 1950, $13-15)

Arthur Eads and his wife Mary Ruth operated the Midway in 1928 and then moved to the Capitol Restaurant and Barnsdall Station beginning in 1929. They later opened the Eads Café in the heart of Cuba. The Eads later became the B and M Café, housed the Jesus Christ Foundation, and now is occupied by a salon. *Courtesy People's Bank Archives* (1930s)

The Hotel Cuba was originally named the Palace Hotel, constructed in 1915 with its entrance facing the Frisco tracks. An entrance facing Route 66 was constructed in the 1930s. In 1946, AAA said the Hotel Cuba was the "best available." It was owned by Mr. and Mrs. S.B. Livingston when this view was made. The building was damaged by fire and condemned in November 2009. (1941, $8-10)

Cuba is known as "Mural City U.S.A." for its colorful murals highlighting area history. Looking east on the future Route 66 (Washington Boulevard) at Smith Street, the People's Bank Building is at right. H.H. Tieman's general store is across Smith Street at right, known as "Prosperity Corner." It is now the Hayes Shoe Building and is adorned with a mural recreating that popular early 1900s gathering spot. (c. 1910, $60-65)

Scherer's Café was one mile west of St. James. "Pop" Scherer said, "We Never Close. We serve everything in season with no substitutes. Popular prices, plenty of parking space." A larger building was later constructed, and then moved to the Jamestown golf course in December 1964. (c. 1945, $25-30)

The American Way Court in Saint James advertised "Modern, heated cottages. Cool in summer. City water. Catering to travelers wanting clean, respectable accommodations at reasonable rates. Open all year." It was later known as the Stanley and K Cottages and still stands today. The units are now rented by the month. (c. 1940, $35-40)

Mr. and Mrs. Roy Finn owned Finn's Motel. "Rest with us tonight, to drive your best tomorrow. Marvelous beds, very clean, free room T.V., air-conditioned, ceramic tile bath, beautiful furniture, and individual thermostat controlled heat." The motel is still in business today, although the cool sign has been replaced. (c. 1960, $6-8)

Vineyards and grape stands line Route 66 through Rosati, originally known as Knobview and settled by Italian immigrants. In 1934, the community was renamed in honor of the first bishop west of the Mississippi, Joseph Rosati of St. Louis. The Marchi Family stand is shown here. *rosati-mo.com* (1964)

The six Rock Haven cabins were constructed in 1926. Frank and Ruth Waring took over in 1950, adding a gas station and restaurant. They sold to Rudy Gilder in 1954 and he ran the complex until I-44 came through. The Rock Haven later became a nightclub and tavern. The restaurant is now a private home and one cabin still stands. (c. 1946, $25-30)

Pierce-Pennant Petroleum Company offered the first high class facilities for Ozark motorists and pioneered the use of radio advertising and free maps. The Rolla Pennant Hotel opened on November 4, 1929. Rowe Carney took over in 1942. It was remodeled into the Manor Motel in 1963 and demolished in 1970. (c. 1960, $8-10)

Toky's Bar-B-Q was "three miles east of Rolla, opposite the Rolla Airport." The back of the card reads, "Nationally known for Bar-B-Q Chicken, Ribs, Pork, Beef. Air Conditioned Dining Room. Curb Service. Orders to go." The restaurant closed in the early 1970s. (c. 1957, $6-8)

The Colonial Village opened in 1937, owned by Mrs. Lorene Lavery. The hotel had 24 rooms with cabins in the back. Later Hull's Colonial Village, it advertised "Food You'll Long Remember." It was known as Frederick's from 1963 to 1976, and torn down in the 1980s. Lee's Fried Chicken was constructed here. (c. 1950, $6-8)

The Pennant Tavern opened on August 1, 1928. Mr. and Mrs. R.W. Martin, former owners of the Wagon Wheel in Cuba, turned it into the Pennant Café and Hotel Martin in 1946. After a fire on August 15, 1953, part of it was incorporated into a new Martin Motel. The Budget Deluxe Motel is located on this site today. (1946, $13-15)

Rowe Carney owned the Rolla Drive In, as well as the Ritz, Rollamo, and Uptown Theatres. In 1956, he opened the Carney Motel near the Pennant, advertising "Service You'll Like and Remember." Each room had large picture windows with an "unequaled panoramic view," overlooking the new four-lane Route 66. (c. 1957, $4-6)

R.E. Schuman opened his Cottage City about 1928, and local lore says some of the 17 cabins were converted chicken coops. It grew into "Tourist City" (later Motor City) with accommodations for over 100 people. The site became the Budget Motel, now the Budget Apartments. (c. 1950, $12-15)

Looking east from the intersection with Pine Street (City 66), Schuman's Tourist City is on the left with the Bell Cafeteria and Pickwick Bus Station on the right. The Pennant Tavern is also visible on the right. The artist took some liberties, removing a stop sign, phone poles, and a stoplight. But a nice sunrise was added. (1946, $12-15)

John Mullen operated the Midway Garage and Star Café in the 1920s. Allyne Earls took over the Midway in 1934, and even had a fleet of taxis. The doors never closed and no one could find the keys when she sold in 1972. Noel Picard, St. Louis Blues hockey player and broadcaster, owned the Midway from 1976 to 1983. (c. 1950, $10-12)

The Trav-L-Odge Tourist Court was originally the Ozark Hills Tourist Court, built when the road was still Missouri Route 14. It took the name well before the Travelodge chain was incorporated, but the back of this card was stamped "Not connected with Trav-elodge Corporation." It later became the Rolla Motel. (c. 1950, $13-15)

Looking east from the U.S. 66 and 63 (Bishop Avenue) at City 66 (Kingshighway) Route 66 curves to the left and City 66 heads straight past the large letters spelling out "Rolla." There was a similar sign at the east entrance to City 66. This area developed quickly after World War II. (c. 1940, $35-40)

The Phelps Oil Company's Modern Cottages, originally the Rolla Courts, were "One of the finest auto courts in the Ozarks." The card reads, "Sleep where sleeping is safe. 16 modern, steam-heated and air-conditioned fireproof cottages." It was later named Grande Court and the site is now a Dairy Queen. (c. 1950, $13-15)

A string of businesses sprang up during the 1950s at the junction with the new four-lane Route 66. They included Zeno's, the Rolla Rancho Motel, Bypass Motel, and Dickmann's Wayfarer Inn. The Skillet Café, operated by Mrs. L.G. Fitwater, was immediately to the east of the Wayfarer Inn. (1958, $10-12)

City Route 66 in Rolla used Pine Street and 6th Street to Kingshighway. Looking north on Pine at 8th Street, clockwise from top right are: the Ben Franklin store in the Schuman Building; Hotel Edwin Long; Scott's Drugs, which was in business here for almost 75 years; and the Moran Building, where Bank of America is located today. (1959, $4-6)

M. E. Gillioz named his Hotel Edwin Long for a senator who died in 1928. It hosted the celebration marking the paving of Route 66 across Missouri just three days after opening on March 12, 1931. The First National Bank of Rolla was on the first floor. Phelps County Bank took over the entire building in 1963, and it was restored in 2001. (1955, $8-10)

Paul and Gladys Bramwell Bennett's café, famous for catfish dinners, opened in 1943 just west of the Newburg Road. (Route T) Paul was a preacher who held camp meetings out back. The four-lane construction forced Bennett's to move to Clementine in 1952. That location closed in 1962 due to I-44 construction. (c. 1946, $40-45)

The Ozarks

West of Rolla, Route 66 drops 425 feet into the valley of the Little Piney River. Route 66 and Interstate 44 have been re-aligned several times in an effort to ease the steep grades. This is one of the most scenic areas on all of Route 66, with densely wooded hills and narrow valleys cut by crystal clear streams. Don't miss the original 1920s route through the resort community of Devil's Elbow. After passing the entrance to Fort Leonard Wood, the highway winds into Waynesville.

In 1941, the *Missouri WPA Guide* described Waynesville as "unmarred by the smoke of industry and the impatient panting of trains, and but little jarred by farmers' Saturday night visits or meetings of the county court." That changed with the construction of Fort Leonard Wood. Route 66 then passes through Buckhorn and Laquey (pronounced "Lakeway"). Hazelgreen is a popular resort area, offering fishing and float trips on the pristine Gasconade River.

Arlington, originally known as Little Piney, was a popular resort for sportsmen on the Frisco Railroad decades before Route 66. I-44 construction left what remains of Arlington tucked away on a dead end service road. Rowe Carney bought the entire community in 1947 and created an RV park here about 1970. (c. 1910, $4-6)

Over the years, Arlington has been part of St. Louis, Gasconade, Crawford, Pulaski, and Phelps Counties. It was even the Crawford County seat for a short time. The James Harrison House was constructed about 1818 and served as the first Crawford County courthouse. It was torn down for construction of four-lane Route 66. (c. 1940, $20-25)

Stoneydell Swimming Pool was the most lavish roadside stop made of native rock. Constructed by George Prewett and a Mr. Andres in 1932, a waterfall provided fresh water from three artesian wells. Fred and Esther Widener took over Stonydell in 1954. Everything shown here was torn down for I-44 construction in 1965. (1932, $100-125)

In 1936, newlyweds Nellie Munger and Emmett Moss opened a sandwich shop east of the Devil's Elbow Bridge. Jessie and Pete Hudson took over, and then moved their business to Lebanon after Devil's Elbow was bypassed. In 1946, Paul and Nadine Thompson renamed it the Elbow Inn. It closed in the 1960s but reopened in 1997. (c. 1940, $55-60)

The communities of Clementine and Hooker were listed in many travel guides as "Basketville," for the handcrafted baskets sold by locals along the highway. Squire and Anna Wells started this station and souvenir stand, where the entire family turned out baskets. This building was destroyed by fire in 1945. (c. 1940, $45-50)

After the fire, Sterling Wells moved to the new four-lane and opened his Hillbilly Store, famous for 19 cent hamburgers. The business moved again when I-44 opened, and then closed in 2000. The hillbilly with rotating arms ended up in Willow Springs, Missouri. A similar one built for the I-44 location is now at the Mule Trading Post. (c. 1967, $10-12)

The treacherous, winding original alignment of Route 66 through Hooker and Devil's Elbow couldn't handle the massive increase in traffic when Fort Leonard Wood was constructed. The Hooker Cut on the four-lane constructed in 1942 was the largest in the U.S. at the time and became a favorite subject for postcards. (1946, $2-4)

The State Planning Commission in 1941 named Devil's Elbow one of the Seven Beauty Spots of Missouri. The name was bestowed by frustrated lumberjacks trying to float tie rafts around a sharp bend on the Big Piney River. Dwight Rench ran Cedar Lodge and the Devil's Elbow Café beginning in 1932. The cafe burned in 1974. (c. 1940, $4-6)

The Devil's Elbow Motel was built by the McClary family in 1951 where the old two-lane alignment meets the four-lane west of the Big Piney River. "New – Clean – Modern – Heated – Air Conditioned. Member AMHA." It was used as rental property after I-44 was constructed, but is now crumbling. (c. 1955, $6-8)

This bridge over the Big Piney River was part of the new highway constructed during WWII to speed men and equipment to Fort Leonard Wood. It was the first major four-lane section of Route 66 in Missouri to be constructed and the last to be bypassed. I-44 here opened in 1981 and the bridge carries Route Z traffic today. (c. 1946, $2-4)

On December 3, 1940, the Army broke ground on a major training facility that wiped out small communities such as Bloodland, Cookville, Tribune, and Wharton but launched a boom for the rest of Pulaski County. It is named in honor of Major General Leonard E. Wood, Army Chief of Staff from 1910 to 1914. (1940s, $6-8)

James Egan's Wagon Wheel Station and Café opened in the early 1920s and expanded with the construction of Ft. Leonard Wood. It was open around the clock. The building later became a popular nightclub but was torn down. The site is now part of the Ramada Inn property. (c. 1948, $60-65)

The turnoff to Ft. Leonard Wood was quickly jammed with traffic and lined with taverns and dance halls. The number of vehicles passing this point every 24 hours soared from 119 in 1939 to 16,375 in March 1941. Crashes on "Bloody 66" in Phelps, Pulaski, and Laclede Counties took 54 lives during the first nine months of 1941. (1941, $30-35)

The Mark Twain Motel six miles east of Waynesville was constructed in the early 1950s and took its name from the nearby Mark Twain National Forest. It advertised "26 units – Air Conditioned – T.V. in All Rooms – Wall to Wall Carpeting – Tile Baths. Restaurant 6 a.m. until midnight." (c. 1956, $4-6)

The Ranch Motel was billed as the closest motel to Fort Leonard Wood and was constructed at about the same time. Note the name of the motel spelled out in the landscaping. The exterior was later covered with stone and the motel remains in business today. (c. 1957, $4-6)

Jody and Hermann Paulette are shown in front of their café, which opened in 1943. They specialized in home cooked meals and hot biscuits served 24 hours a day and "Your Favorite Drinks served in the adjoining Elbow Room." Jody's was located just west of where Mid-America Motors stands today. (1957, $10-12)

Mr. and Mrs. Leo Ablin's Park N Eat advertised "Home of the world's largest hamburger. Curb service – large dining room. Food prepared in sight must be right. From a hamburger to a complete meal. Specializing in steaks – Bar-B-Q – chicken – sea foods – sandwiches – complete fountain service." The restaurant burned down in the 1970s. (c. 1956, $10-12)

In 1940, Neil "Doc" Williams built the Oakwood Village after he somehow found out about the construction of Fort Leonard Wood ahead of time. It may have been a coincidence that Senator Harry Truman was his friend. Oakwood was demolished in 1960 for construction of the I-44 interchange. (c. 1940, $30-35)

The original Tut's Café, known for charcoal broiled steaks, was located on North Street behind the courthouse in Waynesville. Tut's Café Number Two was constructed to take advantage of the new four-lane highway and was located one mile east of town. Cabins were available at the second Tut's location. (1950, $55-60)

The Old Stagecoach Stop on the east side of the Waynesville square is the oldest structure in Pulaski County. Constructed in the 1850s, it was used as a hospital by Union troops during the Civil War and then enlarged into a hotel. It was condemned in 1982, but a foundation was organized to save and restore the structure. *Courtesy of Terry Primas* (c. 1885)

The Old Pulaski County Courthouse was built in 1903 and served as the courthouse until 1989. It now houses the very interesting Old Courthouse Museum. In 1990, this was one of three stops made by Missouri Governor John Ashcroft to mark the signing of a measure designating Route 66 as a historic roadway. ($8-10)

Claude and Eva Rigsby opened a gas station next to their home in Waynesville about 1923. The family ran the station and the small beauty parlor on the left for about 33 years. The Rigsby home is now a restaurant. The gas station building still stands as well, but has been remodeled. *Courtesy of Terry Primas* (c. 1951, $60-65)

Waynesville was established in 1833 as a trading post for settlers and trappers and named for Revolutionary War hero General "Mad" Anthony Wayne. The Union built a fort here to protect the Wire Road during the Civil War. Bypassed by the railroad, the town grew slowly until the construction of Ft. Leonard Wood. (1931, $13-15)

Lawyer and judge Robert A. Bell expanded the family home into a hotel in 1925. The Bell family operated it until 1937 and it was later operated by Mr. and Mrs. Norman Coleman, promising "Old Southern Hospitality." The building is now the Memorial Chapel of Waynesville funeral home. (c. 1935, $13-15)

The Bell family also ran a Standard station, garage, café, and camp next to their hotel. Mr. and Mrs. W.L. Thomas later operated it, but kept the Bell name. On the back of the card, they invited travelers to "Sleep in Safety and Comfort." The service station still stands, and is now Every Bloomin Thing Florist. (c. 1940, $13-15)

Walt and Mildred Preslar's Tasty Grill was across from the Ft. Wood Theatre. It opened in 1951 and had red tile floors with red booths. The grill was open around the clock, serving all-you-can-eat fried chicken dinners for $1.25 and hamburgers for 25 cents. Walt died in 1977 and Mildred ran it until 1985. The building is gone. *Photo courtesy of Rick Preslar.*

Lucille and William Ransdall operated the Owl Café beginning in 1943. It was later operated by the Long family as the Long Cafe. The building became part of Mallow's "Super Way" Market. The Market is closed, but was still standing in 2009. (c. 1946, $60-65)

The five span concrete arch bridge over Roubidoux Creek was constructed in 1923. It replaced the steel span constructed in 1911 at North Street. A nearby field was a camping spot on the Cherokee Trail of Tears. The pilings for the old bridge are visible on the west side of the Roubidoux, in the RV park. (c. 1930, $6-8)

The D and D Market at Buckhorn was operated by brothers Elmer and Don Duetschman from 1948 until 1972, located where I-44 and MO 17 intersect today. The site is now a convenience store on the south side of the Interstate. No one was seriously hurt in this crash. Note that gas was selling for 12 cents per gallon. *Terry Primas and Ruth Deutschman* (c. 1948)

Ed Lentz constructed the Central Motel and Restaurant in 1951 but was forced to relocate in 1956 due to construction of the new four-lane. He opened this service station and restaurant at Missouri Route 133. Ed was cut off by I-44 and forced to relocate again. That location became the Oasis Truck Plaza. (1957, $10-12)

Hamilton's Pleasant Grove cabins opened in 1932. There were originally five cottages with cooking facilities renting for $1 and $1.50. Rudy and Clara Schuermann later owned the property. The Bell family took over in 1948 and renamed it the Bell Haven Court. It is now a private residence. (c. 1950, $30-35)

Ronald and Minnie Toops opened their souvenir shop one mile south of Buckhorn in 1947. The community took its name from the Buckhorn Tavern, a stagecoach stop on the old Wire Road that had a pair of deer horns on the sign above the door. Toops Ozark Souvenirs closed in 1956. (c. 1950, $25-30)

Frank Jones built the Gascozark Cafe in 1931, coining the name by combining "Gasconade" and "Ozark." He also operated the Gascozark Hills resort on his nearby 300-acre ranch. Rudy and Clara Schuermann later operated the cafe. It became the Spinning Wheel Tavern in the 1950s and is now abandoned. (c. 1946, $60-65)

The Normandy, across from Toops Souvenirs, opened in 1932. It included a hotel, gas station, and restaurant. It later became a pretty wild roadhouse. The Normandy closed during the 1970s and burned down accidentally as volunteer firemen were using it for practice in 1978. The site is now a quarry. *Judy McMurtry and Terry Primas* **(c. 1941)**

Lebanon to Springfield

Lebanon is the largest town on Route 66 between Rolla and Springfield. It was originally known as Wyota. In 1868, when the railroad was built a mile away, the residents simply moved the town. Lebanon is home to the famous Munger Moss Motel and Bennett Spring State Park is just off Route 66. Past Phillipsburg, the old route is far removed from the roar of the Interstate, passing through quiet farmland and small towns on the way to Marshfield. Marshfield, the Webster county seat, was named after the Massachusetts home of Daniel Webster.

This bridge over the Gasconade River was constructed in 1922 and carries service road traffic today. At 271 winding miles, the Gasconade is the longest river entirely within Missouri. The entrance to the Riverside Resort is at the upper left. Riverside opened in 1931 and was torn down for construction of the four-lane in 1956. (c. 1950, $4-6)

Mr. and Mrs. Loren Attoway operated the Satellite Café and Leroy Hawkins sold Phillips 66 products at the Space Station, where a sign shaped like a rocket greeted travelers. The Attoway's stated, "Our Desire is to Make Your Trip a Very Pleasant One" with a "Free Picnic Area with Shady Tables." The café burned in 1999. (1965, $6-8)

The Vesta Court was constructed about 1937 and operated by Clayton Lein from 1942 until 1957. Marie and Bill Williams changed the name of the 23-unit complex to the El Rancho Court. It was demolished after the construction of I-44. The arch over the entrance was relocated to the entrance of the B & D Truck Port. (c. 1946, $35-40)

Dennis Scott built Scotty's Tourist City in the late 1940s. It consisted of a small café, three cabins, and a Skelly gas station. Scotty reportedly managed it from his car for a time. A look inside the café showed it was nothing fancy. Southern fried chicken for $1 was the most expensive of the 10 items on the menu. (c. 1946, $55-60)

Charles Clark's Rock Court opened in the 1930s and was later operated by Fred Parthier. "Strictly Modern Rock Cabins among the trees. Rock Court Café, Famous for Good Food. Chicken and Steak Dinners Their Specialty. 24 Hour Texaco Service." Fire destroyed the station and café in 1965. (c. 1955, $6-8)

Ray Coleman and Blackie Waters opened the 4-Acre Court in 1939. Each cabin had a fireplace and a campground was located to the west. They advertised, "After a Long Day's Drive – A Clean Motor Inn for Comfort and Convenience." One of the cottages burned in 2003, but the rest are rented out as apartments. (c. 1955, $6-8)

The Motel 66 opened about 1940 and was originally known as Weideman's Court. Mr. and Mrs. A. J. Lowry and Mr. and Mrs. Adrin Lowry Jr. owned it when this view was made. "Your Home Away From Home on Scenic Highway 66...Main Street of America." It was torn down when I-44 was completed. (c. 1954, $12-15)

G.E. Wrinkle began constructing a two-story hotel in 1946, but fell ill after one story was completed. His son Glenn established Wrink's Market in the structure in 1950, and his personality made it a Route 66 landmark. Glenn passed away in 2007 and his son Terry took over the store. Sadly, Wrink's closed in 2009.

The Forest Manor Motel was originally the Green Gables Court, four clapboard cabins operated by Elsie and Lee Kimes. Lee died in 1944 and Elsie ran the court until after Route 66 was relocated in 1954. The cabins were connected and additional rooms added on to create the Forest Manor, which is still in business today. (c. 1962, $3-5)

Bowling Alleys on Route 66 included Crestwood Bowl in Crestwood, Meramec Lanes in St. Clair, Colonial Lanes in Rolla, and the Starlite Lanes in Lebanon with "16 Brunswick Gold Crown Automatic Lanes, air conditioned coffee shop, nursery, teen room and free instruction." The Starlite is still operating today. (c. 1959, $12-15)

Newlyweds Emis and Lois Spears and Emis' parents opened Camp Joy in 1927. An archway at the exit proclaimed, "Teach your baby to say Camp Joy." A young Bob Hope spent the night here and later said he regretted leaving without paying his 50 cents. The Spears family ran the camp until 1971 and a few of the cabins still stand. (c. 1935, $45-50)

Joe Knight's drug store at Commercial and Madison Streets was also the Lebanon bus station. He relocated to Route 66 at Missouri Route 5 because of the massive increase in bus traffic during World War II. One ton of hamburger was reportedly served here in 24 hours during the war. Walgreen's stands here today. (c. 1946, $6-8)

This view of Lebanon looks east from Nelson's Tavern and Hotel. Nelson's originally sold Barnsdall products, advertised by a large green and white sign. Confused motorists often thought "Barnsdall" was the name of the town, so Nelson put up a neon sign with an arrow pointing towards the business district. (c. 1946, $10-12)

O.E. Carter and Ed Lawson ran a couple of gas stations in Lebanon, including one where the Orchard Hill Package Store is today. In 1941, they erected a prefabricated station near the Frisco underpass. The café was added in 1950 and advertised, "We serve to serve you again." The café building still stands. (c. 1950, $20-25)

Rea and Ida Reid bought the 66 Sunset Lodge and turned it into the Capri Motel in 1961. They sold in 1966 and the Shepherd Hills Motel was built on the site. In 1972, the Reids opened a small gift shop at the Shepherd Hills that grew into Shepherd Hills Factory Outlet, a landmark famous for Walnut Bowls and Frankoma Pottery. (1961, $6-8)

The Midway Motel was originally the Midway Camp, opened by the Bramwells in 1929. John and Blanche Shank bought it in 1931. Ed and Rita Hamilton took over management in 1950 and expanded it into the station and motel shown here. "Reasonable rates – Quiet – Off The Highway." (c. 1956, $6-8)

At the intersection of Route 66 and Route J at Conway, S.W. "Sim" Harris owned a home on one corner. He had two more gas stations and a motel on the other corners. His son Barney built a café in 1931 that later expanded to take in dad's Standard Station. The business moved to the new four-lane in 1953, but later burned down. (c. 1946, $35-40)

Kermit and Letha Lowery opened their café and station in 1952 and a friend suggested that the Garbage Can would be a memorable name. The café was known for little 10 cent fruit pies, serving up to 400 each day. The abandoned building still stands on the north side of I-44 at Exit 107. (1957, $25-30)

The 66 Motor Court was operated by F.C. Tucker and his son. The motor court closed quickly after the construction of the four-lane highway a couple of years after this view was made. Not a trace remains at the site, now an open field west at the west end of Marshfield. (1953, $55-60)

Huffman's Ozark Souvenirs was located at Strafford, the only town in the U.S. with two main streets and no back alleys, according to *Ripley's Believe it or Not*. Route 66 was built behind the businesses facing the railroad, so the owners simply built new doors facing the highway. (c. 1950, $55-60)

The Abbylee Court was constructed about 1940 and originally consisted of eight double cabins. This view also shows the café, which burned in 1950. The Abbylee advertised its beautiful location "Among the Trees." It is still there today and the units are rented out by the month. (c. 1948, $35-40)

Doc's Place was originally a truck stop/café and nightclub known as the Anchor, which backed up to the Frisco Railroad tracks. "Manufacturers of fine home-made candies: send for price list. Dealers in novelties, gifts, souvenirs, baskets and pottery. We handle the best products in each line and sell them at lower prices." (c. 1950, $15-20)

Springfield Area and the "Ghost Section"

West of Marshfield, Route 66 crosses the gently rolling Springfield Plateau. The area is also known as Kickapoo Prairie and Strafford is located on land that was formerly a Kickapoo reservation. Springfield, the third largest city in Missouri, is home of the landmark Rest Haven and Railhaven Motels, along with the Shrine Mosque and the headquarters of Bass Pro Shops. A plaque in the public square marks the spot where Wild Bill Hickock killed Dave Tutt over a gambling debt on July 21, 1865. The duel is considered the first classic quick draw gunfight in the West. West of Springfield is a very interesting stretch through the remnants of communities like Halltown, Spencer, Phelps, Rescue, and Avilla, all hit hard by the arrival of the Interstate. This area is known as the "Ghost Section," for the numerous roadside ruins.

Looking west on St. Louis Street from Kimbrough Avenue, Martin Chrysler Plymouth at left is now the Discovery Center. McKnolly Buick and the Colonial Motel are also visible. On the right are Crosby Auto Parts, Dee's Liquor, the Little Chef Diner, the Moran Hotel, and the Woodruff Building. (1953, $10-12)

In 1938, Wallace Otto opened his motel courts with six "all modern fire proof steam heated cottages with locked garages." The Bell family bought it in 1947 and changed the name. In January 1952, Jerome and Leila Carroll took over, and expanded to 16 units. Jerome operated the motel until 1998. One cabin and the office still stand. (c. 1946, $13-15)

Floyd Pamplin's Deluxe Courts opened in 1930. "All strictly modern cottages with free lock garages. 36 units. Furnace heat and refrigerated air-cooled. With or without cooking facilities." It became the Ramsey Courts, then Terrace Courts Motel, and then the East 66 Tourist Courts. Furniture Outlet is now on this site. (c. 1951, $10-12)

Art Lurvey was the brother of Burt Lurvey, operator of Lurvey's Motel. Art opened a wood frame nightclub a mile west of Lurvey's in 1942. He later "rocked" the building and opened the Rock View Court in 1953. "17 units – Tub & Shower – Beautyrest Foam Pillows." Lurvey Plaza is located here today. (c. 1955, $6-8)

The Rock Village was constructed in 1947 on the southwest corner of Glenstone Avenue (66) and Kearney Street (Bypass 66). The complex advertised "70% air conditioned" and featured beautiful native stone construction with nice use of glass accents. It evolved into today's Springfield Inn. (c. 1950, $13-15)

The Star Terminal Station and Gene Finch's Drive-In was a popular spot, with music piped outside and evening dances. Pop Locke of the neighboring Eagle Tourist Court once blasted the speakers with a shotgun. Gene guaranteed the food, "If not satisfied WE PAY the check." Note the menu prices on this card. (1941, $25-30)

Mr. and Mrs. Rex G. Wilson operated the Cortez Motor Court from 1940 until 1946. They advertised "All new, modern, heated cottages, kitchenette, single and double. Rooms at popular prices. Coffee shop on grounds" and a cafe "nationally known for food at its best." The Wal-Mart Super Center occupies this site today. (1951, $13-15)

The beautiful rock buildings of the Trail's End Motor Court, two blocks west of the 65-66 Junction on the 66 Bypass Route, were constructed in 1949. It was owned by Mr. and Mrs. W.M. Curtess, and later by J.H. Miller. The Indian that topped the sign is gone, but the buildings still stand and are used as apartments. (c. 1964, $4-6)

The Satellite Motel (now the Raintree Inn) opened in 1959, with a design that perfectly captured the era of the Space Race. "27 Modern Units – Hot water heat and air conditioning with room thermostat – carpeted – ceramic tile bath – Free T.V. – heated swimming pool and playground – adjoining restaurant – good food." (c. 1964, $4-6)

Howard Williams owned and operated the Maple Motel, which opened in 1947 and later became the Maple Motor Court. The motel, torn down in 2006, advertised "Choicest Accommodations. Electrically Heated. Air Cooled or Air Conditioned. Ceramic Tile Baths. Tree Shaded Lawn." (1959, $6-8)

The New Haven Courts opened in 1938 and originally had 12 cabins. Mr. and Mrs. Otis Duggins invited you to "sleep safely" in cabins that were "Strictly modern – fireproof – steam heated by Central Plant – air cooled." In 1946, AAA said the cabins were "very good." (c. 1940, $12-15)

The South Winds Motor Court, "Where nice people stay for rest," opened in 1947 and was owned by Mr. and Mrs. Henry Bugg. "Native Stone Cabins. Automatic Gas Heat. Refrigerated Air Conditioned, Bath and Showers, Air-Foam Mattresses. 35 Units, Newly Decorated." It became the Roy Rogers Motel in 1961 and was demolished in 1970. (c. 1955, $10-12)

In 1953, the New Haven Courts transformed into the Ship and Anchor Motel. The stone cabins were remodeled and connected, and additional construction brought the total to 34 units. "Close by – Dinner House – Cocktail Lounge – Coffee Shop – Shopping Center." It became the Ozark Motel in 1981 and was torn down in 1999. (c. 1955, $5-7)

The White City Tourist Park occupied this site from 1927 until 1946. The Motel Americana opened here in 1959. It became the Flagship Motel in 1981 and is still in business today. "Room Phones, Refrigerated, Steam Heat, TV. Family Units, Commercial Men Welcome." (c. 1964, $4-6)

The Greystone Cottage Court opened in 1949, and the name was later changed to the Glenstone Cottage Court. It is still in business today and still looks much the same. This card advertises "14 units, 4 with kitchenettes. Automatic heat, TV and air conditioning. Picnic and Play Area." (1961, $6-8)

The Skyline Motel opened in 1949 in "The Heart of the Ozarks" and advertised "T.V. – Telephones – Refrigerated Air – Steam Heat. Restaurant and Dinner House Nearby." The stone cottages were later connected and covered with siding. The motel was demolished in 2004. (c. 1957, $8-10)

The Sixty-Six Modern Motor Court was originally Uncle Charlie Haden's Motor Court, opening in 1945. It became the Sixty Six in 1949, operated by Benjamin and Ora Dickey. "AMHA and TRIP TIPS approved." It became the Heart of the Ozarks Motel in 1954 after E.R. Grainge took over and was demolished in 1971. (c. 1955, $10-12)

The Lily-Tulip Corporation chose Springfield as the site for their new plant in December 1951. The plant, with its giant "cup" entrance, employed up to 1,200 people at one time. Sold to Owens-Illinois in 1968, it was purchased by the newly formed Lily-Tulip in 1981 and became Sweetheart Cup in 1989. (c. 1960, $1-3)

Big Al Murphy's Big Boy's Auto Court was constructed in 1937. "Same owner for 16 years. Twelve units, strictly modern, some with frigidaires and cooking facilities. The sign out front said "Hi there. Stop. We've been looking for you today." The Brown Derby International Wine Center now stands on the site. (1953, $15-20)

The Elmhurst Motel on St. Louis Street opened in 1946, offering "Ultra-Modern Cottages with Innerspring Mattresses on Hiways 65 and 66 (City Route) only 3 minutes from Center of Shopping and Theatre District. Recreational Facilities for the Entire Family." It was torn down in 1966 for Dillon's Supermarket. (c. 1950, $8-10)

John T. Woodruff built the Kentwood Arms Hotel in 1926. Woodruff also built his landmark office building on the square, the Colonial Hotel and the Sansone Hotel, all on Route 66. He was also the first president of the U.S. 66 Highway Association. Missouri State University acquired the Kentwood Arms in 1984. (1946, $6-8)

The Shrine Mosque was dedicated on November 3, 1923, built by the Abou Ben Adhem Temple and designed by Heckenlively and Mark. It now seats 4,750, and has hosted notables such as Presidents Truman, Kennedy, and Nixon, as well as General John J. Pershing, John Philip Sousa, Will Rogers, and Elvis Presley. (c. 1935, $4-6)

The Manhattan Dinner House, "The Home of FINE Food," opened in 1947. "We specialize in Chicken and Steak Dinners, Served Family Style." Mary Opal Ball was the owner when this view was made. The building still stands today on Glenstone, across from the Railhaven Motel. (c. 1955, $10-12)

John and Hazel Baldridge operated their motel from 1939 until John died in 1997. They advertised "We service your car while you sleep." The stone cottages were later connected and remodeled and the name was changed to the Silver Saddle Motel in 1957. It became the Dogwood Park Inn in 1997. (1944, $10-12)

Carl Hamby, who owned a couple of the most popular cafes in Springfield, opened the Restwell Motel in 1947 across from O'Reilly Army Hospital. "Television – Telephones – Steam Heat – Air Conditioned – Carpeted." The Restwell operated until 1986 and a car wash occupies the site at Glenstone and Pythian Street. (c. 1960, $4-6)

The Rockwood opened in 1929 and advertised as the "last station before Joplin," and "One of the finest and most beautiful Courts in City." The court was owned by Mr. and Mrs. Earl Massey and J.W. Crabtree operated the café. It became Ginny Lee's Café in 1969, changed names a few times, and became the Rockwood again in 2008. (c. 1950, $15-20)

The Rock Fountain Court, with its colorful fountain in the middle, opened in 1944. "One of Springfield's best," advertising "Large, spacious grounds, quiet and pleasant, clean and comfortable." Sherman Nutt took over in 1961 and named it the Melinda Court after his daughter. The motel still stands, but the fountain is gone. (c. 1955, $6-8)

The "pie" in the middle of the square was in place from 1913 until 1947. Heer's Department Store opened its new building in 1915; two years after fire swept the northeast part of the square. Heer's closed in 1995. The Landers Building was originally known as the Keet Building and opened in 1915. It now houses state offices. (1920, $6-8)

After the "pie" was removed, Route 66 (St. Louis Street) went straight west across the square to exit as College Street. In 1973, the square was turned into an ill fated pedestrian mall and traffic routed around it. In 1999, the configuration was changed again, and traffic now follows Park Central around the square. (c. 1950, $4-6)

The Colonial Hotel opened on August 1, 1907. Built by John T. Woodruff, it originally had two wings. A third wing was added in 1920. The columns in front were moved to Phelps Park when the street was widened. Doomed by the conversion of Business 66 to a pedestrian mall, the Colonial closed in 1978 and was torn down in November 1997. (c. 1963, $3-6)

The Wishing Well Motel opened in 1947 with 17 Units, "Refrigerated Air-Conditioning, Carpeted Floors, Steam or Electric Heat, Tile Tub or Shower Bath, Television, Restaurants convenient. Children's Playground. Homelike Atmosphere You Will Always Remember." The well is gone, but the motel is still open. (c. 1955, $5-7)

A Sonic Restaurant on the Chestnut Expressway marks the former location of the Sunset Court. It was in operation from the 1940s until 1979. "Nice – Clean – Modern, Good Beds, Innerspring Mattresses. Insulated. Some equipped for cooking. Rates: One person $2.00. Two Persons $3.00. A Good Place to Rest." (c. 1955, $12-15)

From the late 1930s until 1960, this property was known as the Red Bird Motel, "The motel with the tree growing through the roof." The Thunderbird Motel, offered "Family Units – Some Kitchens – All Air Conditioned – Free TV – 24-Hr. Restaurants one block." It was torn down in 1980 and Continental Carbonic is located here today. (1964, $8-10)

Andy's Modern Rock Cottages were in operation from 1946 until 1959. "Twelve Modern Rock Cottages with Accommodations for 44 People." Andy's also offered "Clean, Insulated, Comfortable, Inner Spring Mattresses." It later became a body shop, and much of the complex still stands. (1947, $6-8)

Leonard and Wilma Greer converted their home into the Lone Star Tourist Court in 1944. They advertised "Modern Cabins – Standard Service." The Lone Star was reportedly known for a good selection of penny candy. The Best Budget Inn was constructed on the site in 1990. (c. 1950, $20-25)

Allan Rose built the Camp Rose Auto Court on a hill above Pickerel Creek. When selling the motel in September 1949, Henry Luepkes described it as an "Attractive streamlined Spanish type with native stone construction," situated on a wooded hill five-acre site. It is now a private home. (c. 1955, $13-15)

Camp Lookout was 24 miles west of Springfield. It was described as the "Most Modern on 66" when this view was made. It was also billed as "Your Home Away From Home" and as "Spotlessly Clean." The camp included nine cottages, a café, and a gas station. Only the foundations remain today. (c. 1950, $13-15)

Ben Brewer built six native stone cabins in 1925. By the time Shorty West was operating Graystone Heights in 1939, it had eight cabins and a café. Graystone Heights remained in operation until the completion of I-44 and the buildings are now used by R&S Floral. (c. 1948, $35-40)

Carl Stansbury constructed Log City in 1926 with trees he cut down on the property. Log City carried on a good natured rivalry with the Forest Park Camp across the highway. Each time one of the camps added amenities, its rival across the road added on too. The main Log City building was later enclosed and became a body shop. There were 16 cabins at Log City, a few of which still stand.

Fred Mason established a garage, café, and cabins at Paris Springs, and named it Gay Parita, after his wife Gay. Mrs. Mason died in 1953 and Fred didn't rebuild after the station burned in 1955. Gary and Fred Turner built this replica in 2007. Gary greets Route 66 travelers today, making Gay Parita a must stop on the Mother Road. *Gary Turner* (2008)

The "town" of Spencer consisted of a café, barbershop, service station, and garage owned by Sidney Casey. Note the 1926 steel truss bridge over Johnson Creek in the background. Route 66 was relocated in 1956 and the complex closed down in 1961. The long abandoned buildings are being restored by owners Francis and Mary Ryan. *Francis and Mary Ryan* (1930s)

Carthage, Webb City, and Joplin

Route 66 passes through the heart of the Tri-State mining district, an area that at one time provided one quarter of the world's zinc. Carthage was the home of notorious outlaw Belle Starr and boasts a beautiful courthouse on the town square as well as the only surviving drive in theatre bearing the name Route 66. The community of Carterville was once very prosperous, but was devastated when the mines closed after World War One. Huge piles of chat lined the highway, but some are now being used to fill the old mines. Route 66 passes through Webb City and originally zigzagged over several streets through Joplin, the route shifting due to collapsing mineshafts. Joplin had once been two wide-open, rival mining communities, which combined in 1873. Two officers died in a gun battle with outlaws Bonnie and Clyde in Joplin on April 13, 1933. Today, Joplin is the fourth largest metropolitan area in Missouri.

Joplin's Union Depot was designed by Louis Curtiss, a pioneer in reinforced concrete construction and was one of the first "Prairie Style" depots west of the Mississippi. The first train arrived on June 30, 1911, and the last left on November 3, 1969. An attempt at restoration during the 1980s failed, and it stands abandoned today. (c. 1930, $20-25)

Ernest Jackson operated the Kel Lake Motel from 1955 until 1965 and the motel is still in business today. In the 1950s, Route 66 was re-aligned to follow what is now Missouri Route 96. The Sportsmen's Protective League constructed Lake Kellogg between the old Route 66 and the new highway. (1956, $4-6)

The Lake Shore Motel touted its "Beautiful Location – Good Fishing in Lake Kellogg" and their motto, "Wonderful Rest in Cleanliness." J.K. Brunk was running the motel when this card was issued. By 1964, it had been taken over by Mr. and Mrs. Frank Tucker. The Lake Shore is now the Best Budget Inn. (1955, $4-6)

During the 1930s and '40s mainline Route 66 and U.S. 71 entered Carthage over three viaducts spanning the Spring River and the railroad yards. The route was later shifted to enter Carthage over Central, originally Alternate 66. The $205,000 bridges of the "new mile" were dedicated with a big celebration in June 1930. (1930, $12-15)

White's Court was constructed about 1927 and consisted of a gas station/café building and eight stone cottages. The Scotts bought the court in 1957, enclosed the cottages and garages, and ran it until 1987. They advertised "Café in Connection. We Service Your Car." It is now the Red Rock Apartments. (c. 1950, $10-12)

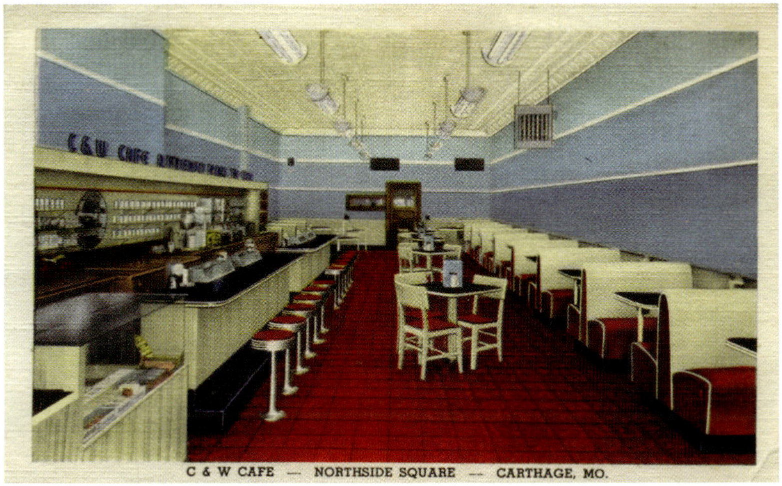

The C & W Café opened in 1935. It was originally on the north side of the square and later moved to the east side. Mr. and Mrs. Bus White and Mr. and Mrs. Ray Carter operated the café, which advertised "A Friendly Place to Eat – Good Food – Moderately Priced – Completely Air Conditioned." (c. 1945, $10-12)

Red Danner's Café opened on August 19, 1941, at Central and Garrison. Red's had a rare 1930s era Chicago Coin bandbox, a coin operated device with miniature foam band figures that play the song *Route 66.* That bandbox is now on display at CD's Pancake Hut, 301 Garrison. (1949, $50-55)

The beautiful Jasper County courthouse on the square is made of Carthage stone, also used for Missouri's State Capitol. The courthouse was dedicated on October 9, 1895. Architect Maximilian Orlop also designed several other lavish courthouses, notably in Dallas, Texas, and New Orleans, Louisiana. (1932, $2-4)

The Ozark Motel had 17 units. It was owned by Mr. and Mrs. Harold Fenix when this view was made, and later by Mr. and Mrs. Herman E. Davis. The card touts "Rubberfoam Mattresses – Air-Conditioned – All Tile Baths." A McDonald's is located here now at MacArthur Drive and Madison Street. (c. 1950, $8-10)

The Lincrest Court and Cafe was described by the owner as "clearing plenty of money" in a newspaper add when it was for sale in June 1946. The back of the card reads "Clean, Cool and Comfortable. One Spot Service – Eat, Sleep and Gas Up. Mr. and Mrs. T.I. Holley, Prop." Some of the cabins still stand. (c. 1948, $12-15)

The Civic Drive-In was the "Tri-State's only Dry Night Club and Restaurant," managed by L.P. Larsen. "Dine and Dance On Our Side Walk Café." The view at the bottom is to the east on Broadway, past the Webb City Bank. The sidewalk café was later enclosed, and the drive-in was converted to an office building. (c. 1941, $30-35)

Bob Miller's first café was at 609 Main. He opened this restaurant at 419 Main on the original site of the Heidelberg Inn after World War II. "The District's Newest – Most Modern – Air Conditioned." Ultra-modern pigmented structural glass was used on the exterior, the counters and the floors. The restaurant closed in 1990. (c. 1950, $8-10)

Looking south from the 400 block of Main Street, the Hotel Connor is on the right. The Joplin Library is located here today. The Keystone Hotel, demolished in 1968, is at left, with the Fox Theatre also visible. Larry P. Larsen designed the Fox, as well as the Civic Drive-In at Webb City. The theatre was converted into a church. (1943, $3-5)

Jay Wilder ran a drug store at 224 Main and then opened his restaurant at 1216 Main. In 1946, he completed a $50,000 renovation that added a 40-foot long mahogany bar. There was an illegal gambling operation upstairs. Clarence Burgraff bought the restaurant in 1977 and sold to Mike and Marsha Pawlus in 1996. (c. 1946, $8-10)

The Twin Oaks Court, "The Place to Sleep," was located just north of the junction with MO 166. It was operated by Fred Beebe and E.J. Friede. They sold to Mr. and Mrs. R.L. Jackson in October 1953, and Mr. and Mrs. W.O. Wistrom later owned it. The Café opened on December 14, 1949, advertising "Just Good Food." (c. 1950, $10-12)

P.H. Carlisle opened the Elms Motel on 7th Street just west of Range Line in 1951. William and Virgil Owen took over about a year later. The Elms advertised "Joplin's finest. 25 beautifully furnished, fireproof cottages on spacious grounds." This view shows the ultra modern lobby. The site is now a shopping center. (c. 1957, $4-6)

The pretty rock East 7th Street Kourts, later the East 7th Street Motel, originally had 17 units and eventually grew to 22. "Individual Air Conditioning. Individual Furnace Heat. Clean, Comfortable, Convenient." Mr. and Mrs. A.C. Jergens were the owners in 1957 and the Bob Owens Auto Center is now on the site. (1957, $6-8)

Harry M. Bennett's Koronado Hotel Kourts were part of an early chain that also had locations in San Antonio and Corpus Christi, Texas. "The Finest and Most Up-to-Date Tourist Kourts in the Entire Southwest on U.S. 66 Highway" had 60 rooms with garages. The Wal-Mart Super Center occupies this site today. (1948, $10-12)

The Joplin Motel on the west edge of the city was operated by Mr. and Mrs. O.T. Bristow and approved by the American Motor Hotel Association. "Rest in the best – Refrigerated Air Conditioned – Private Tile Showers and Tubs – Furnace Heat – A Beautyrest Mattress in every bed. T.V. in rooms." (1957, $6-8)

Roland M. Sharp's Little Kings Hotel Court opened in 1947 at 2207 West 7th. It had 60 rooms. "All New, Latest Improvements, Insulated Walls and Ceilings, Metal Furniture, Box Springs, Venetian Blinds, Storm Doors. Central Heating Plant with Hot Water Heat and Air Conditioning." The motel no longer stands. (1948, $13-15)

Originally the Kastle Kourt, the Castle Motel was owned by Fred R. Prioleau when this view was made. "40 Cottages – Air Conditioned – Phone and Radio in Each Room – Courtesy – Cleanliness – Comfort." It was located on 7th Street 24 blocks west of Main Street, where Fashion Bug stands today. (1953, $12-15)

Since Kansas was a dry state, there were plenty of liquor stores, bars, and nightclubs on the west side of Joplin. They included Dana's Bo Peep, Dixie Lee's Dine and Dance, Ken's Bar, and Dutch's Top Hat. Dutch's featured Missouri's only "completely revolving bar," which could seat 27 people. (c. 1946, $35-40)

W. P. Neff's Liquor and Tobacco Store opened in 1947 on 7th Street, six blocks west of Schifferdecker. It was located across from Harper Airport, the original Joplin Airport, located between 7th and 13th Streets and dedicated on November 11, 1927. Note the totem pole in front of the sign. (c. 1950, $20-25)

An era was ending as this vehicle crossed from Oklahoma into Missouri. The Will Rogers Turnpike opened on June 28, 1957, bypassing all 13.2 miles of Route 66 in Kansas. The view looks east just before the turn-off for U.S. 166 to Baxter Springs, Kansas. 1957. *Missouri State Archives*

Bibliography

American Automobile Association. *AAA Directory of Accommodations.* 1946.

_____. *AAA Directory of Accommodations.* 1954.

Bolin, Norma Maret. *The Route 66 St. Louis Cookbook*. St. Louis: St. Louis Transitions, 2009.

Bradbury, John. *Rolla: The Old Town*. St. Louis, G. Bradley Publishing, 2002.

Curtis, Skip. *The Missouri US 66 Tour Book.* Lake St. Louis: Curtis Enterprises, 1994.

_____. *Birthplace of Route 66 – Springfield MO*. Springfield: Curtis Enterprises, 2001.

Graham, Shellee. *Tales from the Coral Court.* St. Louis: Virginia Publishing, 2000.

Grosenbaugh, Dick. *A Million Hours of Memories. A Condensed History of Springfield, Missouri*. Springfield: Springfield Sesquicentennal Committee, 1979.

Kaszynski, William. *Route 66: Images of America's Main Street*. Jefferson, NC, 2003.

Mann, Dr. and Mrs Clair V. *The Story of Rolla, Missouri.* Rolla Bicentennial Commision, 1975.

Olsen, Russell. *Route 66 Lost and Found*. St. Paul, Minnesota: MBI Publishing, 2004.

_____. *Route 66 Lost and Found: Volume 2*. St. Paul: Voyageur Press, 2006.

Missouri: The WPA Guide to the Show Me State. New York: Duell, Sloane and Pierce, 1941.

Repp, Thomas. *Route 66: The Empires of Amusement.* Lynwood, Washington: Mock Turtle Press, 1999.

Magnan, William B. and Marcella C. *The Streets of St. Louis.* St. Louis: Virginia Press, 1994.

Powell, Jim. *U.S. Highway 66 in Missouri: A Historical Perspective* in *Show Me Route 66 Magazine.* Route 66 Association of Missouri, Fall 2001.

Route 66 Association of Missouri. *Show Me Route 66.* Various issues 1991-2007.

Route 66 Collection. Western Historical Manuscript Collection. Rolla, Missouri.

Scott, Quinta. *Along Route 66.* Norman, OK. University of Oklahoma Press, 2000.

Sonderman, Joe. *Route 66 in St. Louis.* Chicago: Arcadia Publishing, 2008.

_____. *Route 66 in the Missouri Ozarks.* Chicago: Arcadia Publishing, 2009.

Snyder, Tom. *The Route 66 Traveler's Guide and Roadside Companion.* New York: St. Martin's Press, 1990.

Springfield News-Leader. Various issues.

Wallace, Michael. *Route 66: The Mother Road*. New York: St. Martins Press, 1994.

Wickline, David. *Images of 66*. Westerville, Ohio: Roadhouse 66 LLC, 2006.

_____. *Images of 66: Volume 2*. Westerville, Ohio: Roadhouse 66 LLC, 2008.

Witzel, Karl and Gyvel Young. *Legendary Route 66*. St. Paul, Minnesota: Voyageur Press, 2007.